Gender roles and sex equality:
European solutions to social security disputes

Ingeborg Heide

GLOBAL CAMPAIGN ON SOCIAL SECURITY AND COVERAGE FOR ALL

ILO Cataloguing in Publication Data

Gender roles and sex equality: European solutions to social security disputes / Ingeborg Heide; Social Security Policy and Development Branch – ILO, Geneva, 2004

ISBN: 92-2-115771-7
ISBN web version: 92-2-115772-5

PERSONAL AUTHOR: Heide, Ingeborg
CORPORATE AUTHOR: ILO Social Security Policy and Development Branch

ILO DESCRIPTORS: Social security, pension scheme, equal opportunity, equal treatment, Community law, EC country.
ILO FACET: 02.03.1

PHOTOGRAPH COVER PAGE: Staatliche Porzellan-Manufaktur Meissen GmbH, figurine of Greek goddess Themis (Johann Joachim Kaendler, 1745)

Gender roles and sex equality:
European solutions to social security disputes

Contents

List of acronyms

CARDS	Community Assistance to Reconstruction, Development and Stability in the Balkans
COREPER	Committee of Permanent Representations
CFR	Charter of Fundamental Rights of the European Union
DM	Deutsche Mark
EC	European Community
ECJ	European Court of Justice
ECR	European Court Reports
EEC	European Economic Community
EFTA	European Free Trade Association
EOC	Equal Opportunities Commission
EOWM	Programme on Equal Opportunities for Women and Men in the European Union Accession Process
EP	European Parliament
EU	European Union
GBP	Great-Britain Pounds
ILO	International Labour Organization/Office
MISSCEEC	Mutual Information System on Social Protection in the Central and Eastern European Countries Bulgaria, Czech Republic, Estonia, Hungary, Latvia, Lithuania, Poland, Romania, Slovak Republic and Slovenia
MISSOC	Mutual Information System on Social Protection in the Member States of the European Union

Preface

I am very pleased to present this study on *Gender roles and sex equality: European solutions to social security disputes,* the first to be published in a new series on the extension of social security. I hope that it will be a valuable source of information for government officials, social partners, legal experts and all who would like to know more about European equality law. The purpose of this book is to inform the ILO's constituents and legal experts, particularly in the Member States of the European Union and in countries that will accede in the future, about supra-national law on sex equality. The concepts developed at the supra-national level may also stimulate new thinking in other legal systems.

Since its inception, the ILO's mandate has been to improve the conditions of labour by the protection of the worker against sickness, disease and injury arising out of his or her employment, and provision for old age and injury. As early as 1919, in the Preamble to the ILO's Constitution, the protection of women and the principle of equal remuneration were highlighted as areas calling for immediate attention. At Philadelphia, in 1944, the International Labour Conference affirmed the importance of economic security for all human beings and called upon the ILO to promote the extension of social security measures to provide a basic income for all. The Equal Remuneration Convention, 1951 (No. 100), was the starting point for including in the Treaty of Rome the right to equal pay for women and men. This provision has become one of the most relevant legal sources for equality in the field of social security.

In the European Union – like almost everywhere else in the world – women are disadvantaged in terms of income and social security. This is partly a result of the traditional features of the prevalent systems of social security based on the concept of the "male breadwinner". Such systems reflect the traditional division of paid and unpaid work between men and women and are characterized by sex-related distinctions. In addition, women are concentrated in irregular forms of work at the bottom of the income scale and often excluded from access to statutory and employer-financed social security.

This book describes how European law is made and how it operates. It then goes on to deal with the specific instruments and their interpretation by the European Court of Justice. Through its extensive case law on occupational and state pensions, the European Court of Justice has developed an innovative approach to addressing direct and indirect discrimination. The Court has declared equal pay and equal treatment to be fundamental workers' rights which must be interpreted broadly. It has modified the burden of proof and thus increased the chances for an individual to win a case. It has also reinforced the obligations of the Member States to provide effective protection and compensation. Knowledge of supra-national law and the machinery to enforce it is essential to overcome sex-related disadvantages. This book therefore provides a checklist for legal practitioners and a list of the relevant Social Chapter of the Treaty and legislation.

I would like to express my sincere thanks to Ingeborg Heide who developed the concept for this publication and undertook the analysis of European law and practice. I am convinced that those who are responsible for the legislation, implementation, jurisdiction and defence of equality rights in the European region will be greatly helped by her work.

Emmanuel Reynaud, Chief
Social Security Policy and Development Branch
International Labour Office

Acknowledgements

Work on this study was carried out in 2003 and 2004. I received much encouragement from Emmanuel Reynaud (Chief of the Social Security Policy and Development Branch of the International Labour Office), whom I wish to thank for his commitment on gender equality issues and for his unfailing support of the project that resulted in this book.

Thanks also to Amanda Flores for her meticulous proofreading and assistance in finalizing the manuscript, to Angela Haden for her editorial help, to Rosemary Beattie, Wouter van Ginneken and Mark Lansky for their valuable suggestions with respect to the editing and the title. I would also like to thank my colleagues for their useful hints and technical support, in particular Isabelle Bellaton, Guy Bezou, Michèle Bhunnoo, Dominique Blanvillain, Irene Brown, Sandrine Brusseaux, Lauren Elsaesser, Maxime Feroul, Elaine Fultz, Victoria Giroud, Ivon Grether, May Hofman, Martine Jacquinod, Karuna Pal, Sergio Pilowsky, Sabrina Régent, Nathalie Rousseau, and last but not least Xenia Scheil-Adlung.

The cover design is based on a picture of a figurine of the Greek goddess Themis, representing justice (Johann Joachim Kaendler, 1745). This was generously made available by the Staatliche Porzellan-Manufaktur Meissen GmbH (Germany).

Chapter 1: Historical background and political context

1. The European Union at the moment of enlargement

European Community law has fundamentally changed the situation of sex equality in Europe. It applies to the European Union Member States, as well as to Iceland, Liechtenstein and Norway as members of the European Free Trade Association (EFTA). Cyprus, the Czech Republic, Estonia, Hungary, Latvia, Lithuania, Malta, Poland, Slovakia and Slovenia joined the Union on 1 May 2004. Bulgaria and Romania hope to do so by 2007. Turkey is not currently negotiating possible future accession. The Copenhagen Council decided in 1993 that the associated central and eastern European countries which so wished could join the European Union (EU) as soon as they were able to meet the obligations inherent in membership.

Accession countries are required to bring their national systems in line with general European values such as democracy, the rule of law, respect for human rights and the protection of minorities[1]. They need to fulfil economic and political conditions known as the "Copenhagen criteria" encompassing: (a) institutional stability such as to guarantee democracy, the rule of law, respect for human rights and protection of minorities; (b) a viable market economy, as well as the ability to tackle competitive pressures and market forces within the Union; and (c) the ability to fulfil the obligations of accession, including compliance with the objectives of political, economic and monetary union. In addition, they must fully comply with the *acquis communautaire*, i.e. the Founding Treaties, secondary legislation and the case law of the European Court of Justice. These obligations cannot be postponed or be subject to exemption unless specifically permitted in the Treaty of Accession[2].

---

[1] See *European Principles for Public Administration*, SIGMA Paper No. 27. SIGMA (Support for Improvement in Governance and Management in Central and Eastern European Countries) is a joint initiative of the OECD and the European Union; http://www.oecd.org/

[2] *Treaty of Accession of the Czech Republic, Estonia, Cyprus, Latvia, Lithuania, Hungary, Malta, Poland, Slovenia and Slovakia*, signed in Athens on 16 April 2003, see: http://europa.eu.int/comm/enlargement/negotiations/treaty_of_accession_2003/index.htm

The alignment process has been launched on the basis of a "structured relationship" and the *Europe Agreements* concluded between 1991 and 1996 with Bulgaria, the Czech Republic, Estonia, Hungary, Latvia, Lithuania, Poland, Romania, Slovakia and Slovenia, and the former *Association Agreements* with Cyprus (1972), Malta (1970) and Turkey (1963)[3]. The "pre-accession strategy" is supported under the PHARE programme[4] and monitored by the European Commission.

The Commission issues regular reports on the progress made in all relevant fields. In its *Strategy Paper and Report 2002*[5], it pointed out that social policies in some of the applicant countries require further attention, in particular with respect to labour law, safety and health at the workplace, equal opportunities for men and women, anti-discrimination, social protection and coordination of social security. Studies on the level of gender equality achieved in nine of those countries have recently been carried out in the context of the Programme on Equal Opportunities for Women and Men in the European Union Accession Process (EOWM)[6]. They show that significant areas of concern remain *de facto*, despite positive changes in the national standards on equality between women and men. European equality law nevertheless prohibits all forms of direct or indirect discrimination, *de lege* or *de facto*, based on sex. That law must be implemented fully and effectively.

Other countries, particularly in south-eastern Europe, are seeking to align their national legal framework with European law: Albania, Bosnia and Herzegovina, Croatia, the former Yugoslav Republic of Macedonia, and Serbia and Montenegro. At the Zagreb Summit of November 2000, the European leaders decided that the route to stability in that region was through steadily closer association with the EU, with the clear prospect of membership. This policy, known as the stabilization and association process, focuses on the development of privileged political and economic relations, supported by a substantial financial assistance programme (CARDS). The five countries are engaged in ambitious political and economic reform programmes based on Community law and practice. The fight against poverty and social exclusion, which is strongly linked with the level of social protection, will be one of the major items to be addressed[7].

---

[3] Published under: http://europa.eu.int/comm/enlargement/pas/europe_agr.htm
[4] For details see: http://europa.eu.int/comm/enlargement/pas/phare/index.htm
[5] See: http://europa.eu.int/comm/enlargement/report2002/
[6] See: http://www.eonet.ro/
[7] See: http://europa.eu.int/comm/external_relations/see/sap/com02_163.htm

1.2   The role of the ILO in the enlargement process

In his Report to the 87th Session of the International Labour Conference 1999 on *Decent work*, the Director-General of the ILO identified supporting the applicant countries to improve their systems of social protection and equal opportunities as being among the major tasks of the ILO[8]. The European Commission has confirmed its interest in cooperating with the ILO, particularly for the enlargement process, the promotion of fundamental social rights, and social protection[9].

Up to now, most social security systems have reflected features of the "male breadwinner" model. Male breadwinner systems are based on the assumption that the male partner earns a living in paid employment, while the female bears prime responsibility for unpaid household and family work. These systems were originally designed to meet the needs of men and women in a society where the paid and unpaid tasks were rigidly divided between the sexes. A married woman is usually granted a form of protection derived from that enjoyed by her husband; her own earnings are treated as supplementary. Married men, compared with married women, are often disadvantaged with respect to survivors' benefits. However, the role of women in society and attitudes towards family structures no longer correspond to this traditional model. Family structures have changed, and the number of lone parent households is steadily rising. But current legislation, on which social security schemes are based, continues to reflect the idea of the male breadwinner in one way or another.

Women are increasingly present in paid employment but generally acquire lower social security rights than men. Women often work in jobs that are insufficiently covered by social security, such as part-time, low-income, intermittent or precarious jobs, or work at home or domestic work. Even if women have access to social security, they may not fulfil the qualifying periods, or they may not acquire sufficient entitlements to live independently. Inequalities may occur with respect to: (a) the tailoring of rights to benefits and the "individualization" of such rights;

---

[8] See: http://mirror/public/english/standards/relm/ilc/ilc87/rep-i.htm, p. 53.

[9] See Communication from the European Commission "The European social dialogue, a force for innovation and change", *Proposal for a Council Decision establishing a Tripartite Social Summit for Growth and Employment*, Doc. COM(2002) 341 final, 2002/0136(CNS) under http://europa.eu.int/servlet/portail/RenderServlet?search= DocNumber&lg=en&nb_docs=25&domain=Preparatory&in_force=NO&an_doc=2002&nu_doc=341&type_doc =COMfinal

(b) equality of treatment as regards retirement age; (c) the division of pension rights in the event of separation; (d) taking into account the situation of parents with family responsibilities for the calculation of or access to benefits; and (e) the granting of survivors' benefits under equal terms for both partners. Some of the most blatant effects are to be seen in company pensions and health plans.

The topic of sex equality in social security schemes was addressed in Report VI to the 89th Session of the International Labour Conference 2001 [10]. This report traces direct discrimination in the field of social protection to:

> (i) differences in treatment between economically active married women and men, based on the idea that the woman is dependent on her husband, so that her social insurance entitlements are derived rights based on his insurance rather than personal rights based on her own; (ii) differences in rates of benefits or contributions based on actuarial calculations made separately for men and women, taking into account factors such as different life expectancy, risks of morbidity and disability, anticipated work patterns, etc., such differences being found in systems of individual savings accounts in which there is no pooling of risk or solidarity.

The importance of preventing *indirect* discrimination is also stressed in the report. Indirect discrimination is defined as resulting from:

> measures which, although often defined without distinction as to sex, do in practice affect women and men differently because of the nature of their occupational activity, marital status or family situation. Women workers predominate in the sectors not covered by social security, such as domestic, part-time or occasional work or in the informal economy. Certain conditions, such as long qualifying periods, also penalize women.

In 2003, the ILO's Subregional Office for Central and Eastern Europe, located in Budapest, looked at the gender aspect of social security reforms in three of the accession countries: the Czech Republic, Hungary and Poland [11]. It concluded that, although the major reforms undertaken had important implications for women and men, the motivation to achieve sex equality was not often a force in shaping these reforms. In fact, the gender dimension of major policy changes received relatively

---

[10] *Social security: A new consensus,* Geneva, International Labour Office, 2001, p. 69 seq.: http://www.ilo.org/public/english/protection/socsec/download/aconsens.pdf

[11] *The Gender Dimensions of Social Security Reform in Central and Eastern Europe: Case studies of the Czech Republic, Hungary and Poland,* Budapest, International Labour Office, 2003. This study was edited by E. Fultz, M. Ruck and S. Steinhilber and completed as part of the ILO's project supported by the French Government: Strengthening Social Security in Central and Eastern Europe through Research and Technical Cooperation. See: http://www.ilo-ceet.hu/download/gender.pdf

little attention. By virtue of European law, efforts will need to be made. All Member States must fully and effectively implement the Treaties, the legislation adopted on their basis, as well as the case law of the European Court of Justice.

1.3 Europe: Some socioeconomic facts and factors

The social security systems in the Member States are based on different models and reflect history, traditions, cultural heritage and social advances that are specific to each country. Despite these differences, it is a common feature in Europe that social security schemes were originally designed for men as the family breadwinners, working full time without career breaks, and for married women as their dependants, having no continuous working history. This is reflected by direct distinctions made between the sexes concerning contributions and benefits, retirement age and compulsory termination of employment when reaching retirement age, by particular provisions for housewives or male survivors, or by provisions regarding the accrual of entitlements during periods of military service, maternity leave, child care or care for family members. The fixing of minimum waiting periods or entrance thresholds for part-time or temporary workers may lead to *de facto* exclusion of the majority of female workers – a phenomenon of indirect discrimination.

Women increasingly participate in paid employment, but the majority work part time or interrupt their career for unpaid care and family work. In its *Annual Report on Equal Opportunities for Women and Men in the European Union 2002*[12], the European Commission pointed out that the female participation rate in paid employment could be further raised, but that the necessary changes with respect to the cultural and sociopsychological environment seem difficult to achieve. The major reasons for economic inactivity of the population of working age are generally personal or family responsibilities, illness or disability, or participation in education and training. The prevalence of these reasons varies significantly according to sex. Men are inactive mainly because of education or retirement; but almost half of the women aged between 25 and 54 years are economically inactive because of family and household

---

[12] See: http://europa.eu.int/comm/employment_social/news/2003/mar/com0398_en.pdf, p. 9 et seq.

duties. One woman in six does not work in paid employment as a result of family reasons, often because childcare facilities are either insufficient or not affordable.

This picture was recently confirmed by a study on how women and men spend their time[13], carried out in Belgium, Denmark, Estonia, France, Finland, Hungary, the Netherlands, Norway, Romania, Slovenia, Sweden and the United Kingdom. The study found a large disparity with respect to gainful and domestic work. In all the countries surveyed, men devote more time to gainful work or study than to family and household tasks. The time spent by women on domestic work is on average greater than the time spent on gainful work or study in all the countries except Denmark and Norway.

In addition, there are structural differences between the gainful work of men and women – the sexually segregated labour market. Women's jobs are more often poorly paid and precarious than men's jobs. Women work in lower positions and in different sectors. Two-thirds of the employees on low hourly wages are women. Women's wages are, on average, about 84% of men's (87% of male gross hourly earnings in the public sector and 82% in the private sector). Women are disproportionately involved in atypical forms of employment, such as part-time work, temporary work and work at home. They enjoy less job security than men, which makes it difficult for them to have a full-time continuous working history. In the year 2000, 14.5% of women employees, but only 12.5% of men, had temporary jobs. Moreover, the female unemployment rate (10.8%) was significantly higher than the male unemployment rate (7.9%). The sex-related pay gap and sexual segregation in the labour market have hardly changed over the past few years[14].

Such differences cannot be attributed to a single cause, but instances of direct or indirect discrimination would be difficult to deny[15]. In the

---

[13] Eurostat, Press Release 81/2003 of 15 July 2003, see: http://europa.eu.int/comm/eurostat/Public/datashop/print-product/EN?catalogue=Eurostat&product=3-15072003 -EN-AP-EN&mode=download

[14] See: *Report on equality between women and men 2004*, European Commission, http://europa.eu.int/comm/employment_social/news/2004/feb/com_2004_115_en.pdf; http://europa.eu.int/comm/eurostat/Public/datashop/print-product/EN?catalogue=Eurostat&product=3-15072003 -EN-AP-EN&type=pdf; *Employment in Europe 2002*, European Commission: http://europa.eu.int/comm/employment_social/news/2002/sep/employment_in_europe 2002.pdf; http://www.eiro.eurofound.eu.int/2002/10/Feature/EU0210207F.html; Eurostat, *Statistics in focus*, 13/2002.

[15] *Gender Equality Magazine*, No. 11-2001, European Commission, see: http://europa.eu.int/comm/employment_social/equ_opp/gender/mag11-en.pdf; APPLICA sprl, "Earning differentials between men and women - Study based on the Structure of Earnings Survey (SES)", see: http://europa.eu.int/comm/dgs/employment_social/publicat/equ-opp/applica_en.pdf; see also "Gender Earnings Differentials: The European Experience", World Bank 11/1999, http://www.worldbank.org/gender/prr/wp8.pdf; and http://www.eiro.eurofound.ie/2002/01/study/TN0201101S.html (EIRO homepage).

European Union, men are almost twice as likely to be in a managerial position in the private sector than women (10.1 % as against 5.7 %). Only in small enterprises is the disparity between male and female managers less glaring. Women managers make up 2.4 % of all employed, whereas men account for 3.5%. And even in higher posts, women receive less pay than men. A 1997 survey conducted in France, Spain, Sweden and the United Kingdom came to the conclusion that "women bosses fare worst", because the highest pay gap was detected in high positions [16].

In contrast to the situation in the pre-2004 Member States of the European Union, the labour market participation rate of women in the ten accession countries used to be high (except for Malta), but dropped dramatically during the early years of transition. Both women and men have high unemployment levels, especially in Latvia, Lithuania, Malta, Poland and Slovakia. The male participation rate is lower than the average for the pre-2004 European Union, leading to a lower gap between men and women in terms of employment and unemployment; but the labour markets are strongly divided between the sexes, whilst the sex-related pay gap is even wider [17].

A horizontal and vertical segregation of labour markets, combined with a sex-specific working history and pay gap, leads to a further gap in social security rights. Women, more often than men, are excluded *de facto* from access to and benefits from social security schemes, and generally accrue lower entitlements. In Finland, in 2000, women's average total pensions were 841 Euros, 27% lower than men's. In Spain, in 2001, the gap was 37%, with an average contributive pension for women of 405 Euros and for men of 650 Euros. In Austria, in 2000, the average statutory pension was 734 Euros for women and 1,334 Euros for men; in other words, 45% less. In France, in 1997, the average monthly pension for men was 1,342 Euros, compared to 767 Euros for women, amounting to a gap of 43%. In the United Kingdom, in 2001, the pension gap was 16%, with men receiving GBP 183 per week and women GBP 153.

With age, women increasingly outnumber men. Women represent the majority of older people; six out of ten people over 65 years of age and almost two-thirds of the population over 75 years are women. Women of 65 years and over have 10% less income than men in the same age

---

[16] Eurostat 1997, see: http://europa.eu.int/en/comm/eurostat/

[17] See footnote 12. For comparison with countries outside the European region see *The Gender Impact of Pension Reform - A Cross-Country Analysis*, World Bank Policy Research Working Paper 3074, June 2003, under: http://econ.worldbank.org/files/27365_wps3074.pdf

group. The income gap lies between 9% and 12% in most countries, although it is 4% in Spain and around 15% in Finland and the United Kingdom. In 10 pre-2004 Member States, women aged 65 years and over are more likely than men to be at risk of poverty. Around 85% of old people living alone and at risk of poverty are women. The sex difference relating to income beyond retirement age is particularly marked in Denmark, Ireland and the United Kingdom[18].

Certain differences in social security coverage for men and women are acceptable, while others must be regarded as discriminatory by virtue of supra-national law. European Community law prohibits many forms of direct and indirect discrimination, and is often more effective than national law. The following analysis of European legislation (Chapter 2) and case law (Chapter 3) aims to create awareness of the various forms of sex discrimination in social security schemes. It shows that unlawful practices are not rare exceptions, and explains how inequalities between the sexes can be addressed through legal means.

---

[18] Eurostat, Statistics in focus, 21/2002: *Women and men beyond retirement,* see: http://europa.eu.int/comm/eurostat/Public/datashop/print-catalogue/EN?catalogue=Eurostat&product=KS-NK-0 2-021-__-N-EN

Chapter 2: The overall legal framework

2.1 European Community law — Its nature and general features

Matters of sex equality are strongly regulated by European law. The Member States of the European Union are bound by that law, and so are Iceland, Liechtenstein and Norway by virtue of having signed and ratified the European Economic Area Agreement[19]. In so far as binding obligations are imposed on the States, they are supra-national in nature. This means that binding obligations are directly valid throughout the Union, ranking higher than national law and overriding the authority of the individual State. The Treaty of Accession[20] allows no derogation in the field of sex equality; related European law must have been fully and effectively transposed by the date of accession.

In fields where binding obligations do not exist, the design and effectiveness of social protection schemes remain under the auspices of national authorities. In this regard, the Member States keep each other regularly informed via the Mutual Information System on Social Protection (MISSOC/MISSCEEC)[21]. The funding and organization of social protection systems are vital components of the wider employment and social situation. That is why accession countries have been invited to translate the Union's social objectives into appropriate national policies, and to develop and operate sustainable and universally applicable social protection systems in line with the Treaty's objectives. Acceding States must also be capable of coordinating their social policies with those operating in the Union, which are currently undergoing significant reform. The Commission has encouraged the acceding countries to make use of the experience of the pre-2004 Member States, in particu-

---

[19] For details see: http://www.efta.int

[20] See footnote 3.

[21] See: http://europa.eu.int/comm/employment_social/missceec/index_en.html; http://europe.eu.int/scadplus/leg/en/cha/c00007.htm; http://europa.eu.int/comm/employment_social/soc-prot/missoc98/english/f_main.htm

lar by participating in the new Community Action Programme on Social Inclusion[22].

The European Union is a legal construct, composed of the Union and the Community. The Union pursues its aims through an independent body of law, Community law. The correct implementation of Community law requires more than mere technical transposal into national law. The adoption, implementation and enforcement of European law follow specific rules that are laid down in the Founding Treaties and are not comparable to any other system in the world. To make effective use of Community law, practitioners need to be familiar with the different forms of interaction between the supra-national level (the Community) and the Member States, the unique legislative proceedings, the various forms of legislation and implementation, and the specific enforcement mechanisms. These aspects are outlined below.

2.2 The Founding Treaties as primary sources of Community law [23]

The European Community was created by the Treaty of Rome (1957) and originally designated as an Economic Community. The Treaty of Rome was amended through the Single European Act (1986) and the Treaties of Maastricht (1992), Amsterdam (1997) and Nice (2001)[24]. As part of the Treaty of Maastricht, the Union was created through the Treaty on European Union, and combined with the European Community. All these Treaties are described as Founding Treaties and primary sources of European law. Their adoption follows the rules of international law: all Member States must accept and ratify a Founding Treaty according to their particular national requirements. Once the Founding Treaties are in force, amendments can be made only by unanimous agreement under the same requirements. In the past, any progress achieved in a new Treaty was legally irreversible. The Draft Treaty establishing a Constitution for Europe, submitted on 18 July 2003[25] by the

---

[22] See: http://europa.eu.int/comm/enlargement/negotiations/chapters/chap13/ and http://europa.eu.int/eur-lex/en/com/cnc/2002/com2002_0089en01.pdf

[23] For general information see: http://europa.eu.int/eur-lex/en/about/abc/. For future options in the field of sex equality see: http://europa.eu.int/comm/employment_social/news/2003/jul/options_en.pdf

[24] See: http://europa.eu.int/eur-lex/en/ and http://europa.eu.int/eur-lex/en/search/treaties_founding.html

[25] See: http://europa.eu.int/futurum/index_en.htm

President of the European Convention, Valéry Giscard d'Estaing, contains the option for a Member State to leave the Union unilaterally.

A clear distinction should be made between the European Union and the European Community. The Union sets out the framework for political cooperation in the fields of foreign and security policy, justice and home affairs. Supra-national law is made and enforced only on the basis of the Treaty establishing the European (Economic) Community[26], referred to as the Union's first pillar. The Member States have transferred sovereignty either partly or entirely to the supra-national body, the Community, only for the policy fields covered by the Treaty establishing the European (Economic) Community. Both the Union and the Community can act only within the limits of the powers conferred on them by the Founding Treaties, to which Member States have given their agreement through ratification by referendum or by parliamentary vote.

Even for matters that can be dealt with by the Community, the Member States have been cautious in surrendering powers. Only those powers falling under the exclusive competence of the Community have been surrendered without restriction. Where both the Community and the Member States are competent, the "principle of subsidiarity" applies. The principle of subsidiarity means that the Community is entitled to act only where the same goals cannot be sufficiently achieved by the Member States. The "principle of specific conferment of powers" enables the Member States to monitor and control the surrender of powers: the extent of Community powers must not go further than the tasks specifically laid down in each chapter of the Treaty[27]. Nevertheless, the extent to which the Community may act or interfere in national policies is hotly debated in virtually all areas of legislation on labour and social matters.

2.3 The making of secondary Community law

The Community makes and enforces European law through its institutions[28]. The Commission is the driving force; it embodies and upholds the general interest of the Union and of the Community. The President

---

[26] For citation see: http://www.curia.eu.int/en/actu/communiques/index.htm and the *Consolidated Version of the Treaty establishing the European Community* following the *Treaty of Nice*; for changes through this latest amendment see: http://europa.eu.int/comm/igc2000/dialogue/info/offdoc/guidecitoyen_en.pdf

[27] See Article 5 EC.

[28] See Article 7(1) EC.

and Members of the Commission are appointed by the Member States after they have been approved by the European Parliament. The Commission has the right to initiate draft legislation and presents legislative proposals to the Parliament and the Council. As the Union's executive body, the Commission is responsible for the full and effective implementation of European law and acts as the guardian of the Treaties. Together with the European Court of Justice, it ensures that Community law is properly and universally applied throughout the Union.

The Council adopts legislation, either after a hearing of the European Parliament, or in cooperation or co-decision with it[29]. The Council is composed of the national Ministers responsible for a particular matter[30]. Decisions are taken unanimously, or with a qualified majority where the votes are weighted[31]. The President of the Council places an item on the Council's agenda when there seems to be sufficient agreement to make adoption of legislation possible. The Council, a legislative body, must be distinguished from the European Council. The latter consist of Heads of State or Government and the President of the Commission, and meets at least twice a year to give the necessary impetus for development and to establish common policy guidelines[32]. Although of high political importance, the European Council is not directly involved in the legislative process.

Council meetings are prepared by the Committee of Permanent Representations (COREPER), composed of high-level government officials, normally the Ambassador and his or her representative from the Permanent Representations in Brussels[33]. The Committee of Permanent Representations negotiates the outstanding unresolved points in preparation for a Council meeting. Prior to the negotiations in the COREPER, draft legislation is normally discussed by working groups comprising experts sent from the capitals of the Member States.

Both the Council and the Commission are supported by two advisory committees: the Economic and Social Committee, composed of employers, trade unions and consumer organizations, and the Committee of Regions with representatives from local and regional entities[34].

---

[29] See Articles 249 EC et seq.

[30] See Article 203 EC.

[31] See Article 205 EC; for voting after enlargement see *Protocol on the enlargement of the European Union* annexed to the *Treaty of Nice*.

[32] See Article 13 EU.

[33] See Article 207(1) EC.

[34] See Articles 7(2) and 257 EC et seq.

The European Parliament (EP) is directly elected for terms of five years[35] and is involved in the legislative process. Its position had been enhanced with each amendment of the Treaty. In the early years, the European Parliament was merely "consulted". Now, legislation on social and labour issues is adopted either in "consultation"[36] or in "co-decision"[37] with the Parliament, after possible consultation of the social partners[38].

For three decades, legislation could be adopted only by unanimous agreement in the Council. The Single European Act introduced majority voting on social matters, at that time restricted to health and safety at the workplace. The Treaties of Maastricht and Amsterdam later extended majority voting to: (a) working conditions; (b) information and consultation of workers; (c) the integration of persons excluded from the labour market; and (d) equal opportunity and treatment of women and men at work. Legislation in these fields may only "support and complement the activities of the Member States".

No similar restriction exists for "equal working conditions including equal pay for women and men", on which the Community has original competency[39]. Such legislation is adopted in "co-decision" with the European Parliament[40]. Before submitting proposals in the social policy field, the Commission has to consult management and labour on the possible direction of Community action and, in a second step, on the content of an envisaged proposal. The social partners may be entrusted with implementation at the national level, as long as the State retains the ultimate responsibility[41]. Agreements between the social partners organized at the European level can also be adopted as a directive and become a supra-national instrument[42].

The principle of unanimity in the Council is now limited to particularly sensitive or costly areas such as: (a) social security and social protection of workers; (b) protection of workers against termination of employment; (c) collective bargaining; and (d) the protection of workers against discrimination for reasons other than sex[43]. Generally excluded from supra-

---

[35] See Article 189 EC et seq.
[36] See Article 13(1) EC and Article 137(2) EC, requiring unanimous vote in the Council.
[37] See Article 137(2) EC and Article 141(3) EC.
[38] See Article 138 EC.
[39] See Article 141 EC.
[40] See Article 251 EC.
[41] See Article 137(3) EC.
[42] See Articles 138 and 139 EC.
[43] See Articles 13 and 137 (2) EC and Council Directives 2000/43/EC and 2000/78/EC.

national legislation are the issues of pay (except for *equal* pay), the right of association, the right to strike, or the right to impose lock-outs[44].

2.4 Law enforcement through the Commission and the European Court of Justice

Like any entity governed by the rule of law, the Community needs an effective system of judicial safeguards. These safeguards are the Commission and the European Court of Justice. The European Court of Justice is composed of one Judge per Member State and eight Advocates-General[45]. The Judges – like the Commissioners – act independently of the Member State of which they are citizens. The Court's primary and foremost task is to ensure that Community law is interpreted and applied equally in each Member State. In order to fulfil that role, the European Court of Justice has jurisdiction to hear disputes to which the Member States, the Community institutions, companies and individuals may be parties.

The Court determines, with legally binding effect, whether a national rule or practice is in compliance with European law. Its rulings take precedence over judicial rulings in the Member States. There are specific procedures for bringing a case before the European Court of Justice. Only officials of a Community institution, or persons directly and individually affected by a regulation or decision of a Community institution, may institute proceedings before its Court of First Instance. Any other employee who feels discriminated against is required to file a complaint before the relevant national judiciary. The competent jurisdiction is laid down in national law and may be a civil, labour, social or administrative court.

Any national court dealing with a matter must set aside a national provision that it considers incompatible with European law[46]. This duty of the national judiciary is based on Article 10 EC which obliges the Member States to "ensure fulfilment of the obligations arising out of this Treaty". The obligation of the Member States to achieve the results

---

[44] See Article 137(5) EC.

[45] See Articles 221 and 222 EC.

[46] Permanent case law of the European Court of Justice; see, for instance: Case C-33/89, *Kowalska v. Freie und Hansestadt Hamburg*, ECR 1990, p. I-2591; Case C-184/89, *Nimz v. Freie und Hansestadt Hamburg*, ECR 1991, p. I-297; Case C-442/00, *Caballero v. Fogasa*, ECR 2002, p. I-11915.

envisaged by a directive, and their duty to ensure the fulfilment of that obligation, are binding on all the authorities of the Member States. This includes, for matters within their jurisdiction, the courts. In applying national law, a national court is required to interpret it, as far as possible, in the light of the wording and purpose of an existing directive in order to achieve the results pursued. This is valid particularly for legislative provisions which were specifically introduced in order to implement a directive[47].

The most relevant mechanism to ensure universal application and equal interpretation of supra-national law is laid down in Article 234 EC. It confers on the European Court of Justice the jurisdiction for "preliminary rulings" concerning the interpretation of the Treaty, and the validity and interpretation of Community acts. National courts or tribunals have the option of requesting the opinion of the European Court of Justice on any matter where Community law might be relevant. Where national courts function as courts of last instance, they are obliged to request such a preliminary ruling. The consequence of violation of this duty was only recently decided.

In *Köbler v. Republic of Austria*[48], the question was raised of whether or not an individual is entitled to financial compensation when a – judicially independent – national court adjudicates at last instance without the necessary involvement of the European Court of Justice. As a general rule, a Member State is financially liable for the damage caused to an individual by an infringement of Community law under the following conditions: (a) the rule of law infringed must be intended to confer rights on individuals; (b) the breach must be sufficiently serious; and (c) there exists a causal link between the breach of the obligation incumbent on the State and the damage sustained.

On 30 September 2003, the Court delivered its ruling. It confirmed that the rules on State liability apply, in principle, where a national court adjudicating at last instance infringes Article 234 EC. But in view of the specific nature of the judicial function, the infringement can be regarded as "sufficiently serious" only where it is "manifest". In the case of Mr. Köbler, the Court denied a manifest infringement of Community law, because the Austrian administrative court of last instance might have misinterpreted a former ruling of the European Court of Justice on the substance at stake.

---

[47] Case C-185/97, *Coote v. Granada Hospitality Ltd*, ECR 1998, p. I-5199.
[48] Case C-224/01, see: http://www.curia.eu.int/en/actu/communiques/cp03/aff/cp0379en.htm

Roughly one-tenth of the rulings of the European Court of Justice are "infringement proceedings" under Articles 226 EC et seq. This procedure can be initiated by the Commission or another Member State if a State does not comply with its obligations, for instance by not implementing the aims of a directive properly. Before the matter is brought before the Court, the Commission delivers a "reasoned opinion" on which the State concerned can submit observations. If the Commission maintains its view, it lays down a period by the end of which compliance must be ensured. If the State concerned does not comply with the Commission's opinion within the time frame set, the Commission may bring the matter before the European Court of Justice.

Such a ruling on State liability as a consequence of national court proceedings was delivered on 9 December 2003 in respect of Case C-129/00, *Commission of the European Communities v. Italian Republic*[49]. The matter at stake was an interpretation of the Italian jurisdiction which made it excessively difficult for the taxpayer to exercise a right, granted under Community law, to reimbursement of indirect taxes. The European Court of Justice recalled that a Member State can be found to have failed to fulfil its obligations under Community law, even when this failure results from the acts of a constitutionally independent institution such as a national court. If the legislative text in question is neutral with regard to the requirements of Community law, its effect should be determined taking into account the interpretation of the relevant legal provision by the national courts.

Preliminary rulings are the most common proceedings before the European Court of Justice, and they are becoming increasingly frequent. National courts have become more aware of European law, and even the lower courts tend to refer questions to the European Court of Justice, which they are entitled – but not obliged – to do. In addition, a growing number of Community instruments are being adopted and have to be applied. Another reason for the prevalence of preliminary rulings is that infringement proceedings include an initial phase during which many problems can be resolved in a diplomatic way.

The European Court of Justice has strengthened the workers' position in the majority of cases. It does not limit its role to "judicial self restraint" – the mere interpretation of existing provisions – but actively promotes social rights. This practice is based on Articles 2 and 136 EC which

---

[49] See: http://www.curia.eu.int/en/actu/communiques/cp03/aff/cp0348en.htm

entrust the Community with the task of promoting a high level of employment and of social protection, equality between men and women, and the improvement of working and living conditions.

2.5   Fundamental European rights and minimum standards in the social field

The Treaty of Rome guaranteed the "four fundamental freedoms" essential for the functioning of the "common market": the free movement of workers, services, goods and capital. Workers have the right to seek and perform work in all the Member States, free from discrimination with respect to employment, remuneration and other working conditions, as well as social security benefits[50]. The right to "equal pay for equal work"[51] for women and men was included in the Social Chapter of the Treaty right from the start. But the relevant provision was added for economic rather than for social reasons; France, unlike other Founding States, had already ratified the Equal Remuneration Convention, 1951 (ILO No. 100), and feared a distortion of competition unless the equal pay principle was applicable in all Member States. The feminist movement and, obviously, the higher demand for female labour gave new impetus for the important legislation on equal pay and equal treatment for women and men that was adopted in the 1970s[52]. During the 1980s, the opinion gained ground that the common market should benefit workers in general terms, and be backed by the establishment of minimum social standards valid throughout the Community.

While the common market is regulated by harmonization[53], social policies are usually coordinated or regulated on the basis of minimum standards. The social protection of migrant workers and their dependants is secured by the coordination of the entitlement periods aggregated under the laws of the different countries, and by the payment of benefits to the migrant workers and their dependants in their country of residence[54].

---

[50] See Articles 39 and 40 EC.

[51] Now, after amendment: "equal pay for equal work or work of equal value", see Article 141(1) EC.

[52] According to the *Treaty of Rome*, social progress was expected primarily as a side effect of economic growth and not via legislation, see Article 117 EEC, now, after amendment, Article 136 EC.

[53] The reason is that imposing higher standards in one country would lead to a trade barrier incompatible with the common market. It is illegal for a Member State to impose a higher standard unless the State can prove, on the basis of scientific evidence, that the national measure or provision is necessary to respond to "major needs" or to the imperatives of the working environment, see Articles 30 and 95 EC.

[54] See Article 42 EC and Regulation (EEC) No. 1408/71.

Where a certain social level is to be achieved for all workers, this is done via minimum standards. The minimum level prescribed must be implemented throughout the Union, although the individual Member States may opt for higher standards. States have the choice between a high level of social protection or the competitive advantage of low production costs. Legislation on the working environment and working conditions can be adopted only in the form of directives setting "minimum requirements for gradual implementation" (Article 137(2)(b) EC).

The guarantee of equal pay and treatment is not a minimum standard; there is no less or more equality. But the relevant legislation adds minimum requirements aiming at the promotion of equality through certain bodies or procedures (for example, class action, burden of proof, and information of the workers). Such provisions are "minimum standards" regarding which a Member State may provide a higher level of protection.

2.6 Regulations, directives, recommendations: Their legal character and how they work[55]

The Treaty establishing the European (Economic) Community is a primary source of supra-national law. Community legislation and the rulings of the European Court of Justice are secondary sources. Instruments of secondary law are regulations, directives, decisions and recommendations, adopted on the basis of the Treaty. How they operate is laid down in Article 249 EC:

> A regulation shall have general application. It shall be binding in its entirety and directly applicable in all Member States.
>
> A directive shall be binding, as to the result to be achieved, upon each Member State to which it is addressed, but shall leave to the national authorities the choice of form and methods.
>
> A decision shall be binding in its entirety upon those to whom it is addressed. Recommendations and opinions shall have no binding force.

A directive "shall leave to the national authorities the choice of form and methods". Member States are thus free to implement a directive through existing structures and mechanisms, and at different levels – state,

---

[55] For relevant policies see: http://europe.eu.int/scadplus/leg/en/s02205.htm

regional and local. The governments represented in the Council decide upon the legal nature of secondary law; they prefer to use national institutions, rules and procedures, and therefore favour the adoption of directives. Regulations are restricted to common market issues, where the Community has exclusive competence. In the field of social policies, regulations are used to realize the freedom of movement of workers and related social security rights, for instance through Council Regulations (EEC) Nos. 1612/68 and 1408/71.

For social matters, directives are the usual instruments, and indeed for some areas the only admissible instruments. Directives have certain elements in common. They define the specific aims and addressees of the directive in question, and determine deadlines and obligations to be observed at the national level. Each directive imposes on Member States the duty to abolish any legislation or administrative rules that are incompatible with its aims. Access to justice must be enabled for all who consider themselves wronged by failure to comply with a directive. The entry into force is determined, as well as a deadline for transposal to the national level. Each directive states: "This Directive is addressed to the Member States". The Member States are obliged to report, within a specified period, on the measures taken; these measures are subsequently examined by the Commission in view of compliance, and reported to the Council and the European Parliament. The reports are a useful source of inspiration for the implementation of Community law, or comparative labour and social law[56].

The European Court of Justice has frequently been requested to judge whether an individual can invoke direct rights from a directive, even though the directive is solely "addressed to the Member States". The Court has developed various solutions to this legal problem. In the field of sex equality, it tends to derive rights directly from Article 141 EC on equal pay (former Article 119 EEC). Another way is to accord "immediate and direct effect" to specific provisions of a directive. For claims brought by a civil servant or public employee against the State, the latter has the double function of addressee of the directive and public employer. The Court therefore holds the State directly responsible for the full and effective implementation of all provisions of a directive. This jurisdiction is illustrated below by a number of examples.

---

[56] See, for instance, the following reports on Directives 92/85/EEC (Pregnant Workers) and 96/34/EC (Parental Leave): http://europa.eu.int/comm/employment_social/equ_opp/news/pregnant_en.htm and http://europa.eu.int/comm/employment_social/equ_opp/documents/com2003358_en.pdf

Member States are also financially liable if they do not, or do not in time, or do not correctly transpose a directive into national law. The problem of State liability in such a situation was raised in the case of two workers, Ms. Bonifaci and Mr. Francovich[57]. They had suffered a loss of income because the Italian State had failed to implement Directive 80/897/EEC on the protection of workers in cases of insolvency. They therefore claimed compensation from the State. The Court judged as follows: if a State does not implement a directive during the time frame set, it is liable for the damage caused when the aim prescribed by the directive entails the grant of rights to individuals, when the content of rights can be clearly identified by the provisions of the directive, and when there is a causal link between the breach of State obligations and the damage sustained.

Article 249 EC states that recommendations have "no binding force", but does this mean that they have no legal effect? This question was raised in the case of Mr. Grimaldi. He had applied for a pension to the Fonds des Maladies Professionnelles in Belgium, claiming that he suffered from an occupational disease, which the Fund denied. In contrast to Belgian law and practice, *Commission Recommendation 66/462/EEC on the conditions for granting compensation to persons suffering from occupational diseases* characterized his disease as "occupational". The Court declared that, although a recommendation cannot in itself confer rights on individuals, the "national courts are bound to take those recommendations into consideration in order to decide disputes submitted to them, in particular where they are capable of casting light on the interpretation of other provisions of national or Community law"[58]. As a consequence of this highly disputed ruling, all courts in all the Member States are bound to consider even unilateral interpretations by the Commission.

It is thus up to the individual State to decide *how* a directive is applied. However, national law and practice must always cover the full scope of the directive, and implement it in time and effectively. If the aim of the directive is to grant and protect the rights of individuals – which is normally the case – the law must likewise grant individual rights in cases against any public or private employer. In many rulings regarding the *effet utile* of State measures, the Court has held the State liable for insufficient transposition.

---

[57] Joined Cases C-6/90 and C-9/90, *Francovich and Bonifaci v. Italian Republic*, ECR 1991, p. I-5357; see also Case C-140/97, *Rechberger and Others v. Austria*, ECR 1999, p. I-3499 for further interpretation.

[58] Case C-322/88, *Grimaldi v. Fonds des Maladies Professionnelles*, ECR 1989, p. 4407.

2.7 Legal instruments in the field of social security and related case law of the European Court of Justice[59]

The most important provision on sex equality is the Article on equal pay of the Treaty of Rome (Article 119 EEC, now, after amendment, Article 141 EC). This Article applies to all occupational schemes and certain statutory schemes. Its first two paragraphs read as follows:

1. Each Member State shall ensure that the principle of equal pay for male and female workers for equal work or work of equal value is applied.

2. For the purpose of this article, 'pay' means the ordinary basic or minimum wage or salary and any other consideration, whether in cash or in kind, which the worker receives directly or indirectly, in respect of his employment, from his employer.

This Article was followed up by intensive secondary legislation, starting with *Council Directive 75/117/EEC of 10 February 1975 on the approximation of the laws of the Member States relating to the application of the principle of equal pay for men and women* (Equal Pay Directive). The concept of the Equal Pay Directive entails, for the same work or for work to which equal value is attributed, the elimination of all discrimination on grounds of sex with regard to all aspects and conditions of remuneration. Where a job classification system is used for determining pay, it must be based on the same criteria for men and women. Employees wronged by failure to apply this principle have the right of recourse to judicial process to pursue their claims. Member States must abolish all discrimination between men and women arising from laws, regulations or administrative provisions which do not comply with the principle of equality.

Council Directive 76/207/EEC of 9 February 1976 on the implementation of the principle of equal treatment for men and women as regards access to employment, vocational training and promotion, and working conditions (Equal Treatment Directive) aims to put into effect the principle of equal treatment for men and women as regards access to employment (including promotion), vocational training, and working conditions (including social security). With respect to social security, further legislation was envisaged. The directive prohibits any discrimination whatsoever on grounds of sex, either directly or indirectly, particularly with respect to marital or family status. Men and women are granted the same working

---

[59] For legal texts see: http://europa.eu.int/comm/employment_social/equ_opp/rights_en.html

conditions, encompassing conditions of dismissal. Member States must ensure that any laws, regulations or administrative provisions, collective agreements, individual contracts of employment, internal rules of undertakings, or rules governing independent occupations and professions that are contrary to the principle of equal treatment are declared null and void, amended or abolished.

The Equal Treatment Directive was recently amended through *Council Directive 2002/73/EC* of 23 September 2002. It now offers stronger support for employees who feel that they have been treated unfairly because of their sex. Sexual and other forms of harassment are defined and declared discriminatory. As a consequence of the case law of the European Court of Justice, specific provisions for enforcement, compensation and sanctions are included. Member States have to establish agencies with specified powers to promote equal opportunities. Employers need to introduce preventive measures against harassment and victimization, and to issue regular reports on equality. These amendments will have to be transposed into national law by 5 October 2005.

One of the amendments raises concern in view of the fundamental right of access to justice and a fair trial. Article 6(1) of the amended Directive 76/207/EEC allows, as a suitable alternative to independent justice, "and/or administrative procedures". This is problematic in view of the ruling on *Johnston v. Chief Constable of the Royal Ulster Constabulary*[60]. Ms. Johnston was a uniformed police officer in the Royal Ulster Constabulary. Her contract was not renewed, as a measure to protect women, when the carrying of firearms was introduced in that police force. She felt discriminated against and demanded to be trained in the handling of firearms. However, discriminatory acts done for the purpose of safeguarding national security, or of protecting public safety or public order, were excluded from application of the national Sex Discrimination Order.

The European Court of Justice interpreted Article 6 of Directive 76/207/EEC granting access to justice in the light of Articles 6 and 13 of the *European Convention on the Protection of Human Rights and Fundamental Freedoms*. From the guarantee of the right to a fair trial and effective remedy – principles common for all Member States – it concluded that an individual cannot be deprived of the possibility of

---

[60] Case 222/84, ECR 1986, p. 1651.

asserting his or her rights by judicial process. The ruling demands the possibility of access to an independent court or tribunal to deal with any discriminatory act. This right is confirmed in Article 47 of the *Charter of Fundamental Rights of the European Union*[61], which states the right to a "fair and public hearing within a reasonable time by an independent and impartial tribunal previously established by law". The new Article 6(1) must be interpreted in view of these fundamental rights, so that access to an independent court or tribunal is guaranteed.

The specific instrument governing statutory social security schemes is *Council Directive 79/7/EEC of 19 December 1978 on the progressive implementation of the principle of equal treatment for men and women in matters of social security.* It covers the "working population" including workers whose activity is interrupted by illness, accident or unemployment, persons seeking employment, retired or invalided workers and self-employed person (Article 2). This directive applies to statutory schemes that provide protection against sickness, invalidity, old age, work accidents and occupational diseases, unemployment, and "social assistance, in so far as it is intended to supplement or replace the schemes referred to". It does not apply to survivors' benefits nor to family benefits, unless the family benefits are granted by way of increases of benefits due in respect of the risks covered (Article 3). Without prejudice to the protection of women on the grounds of maternity, direct and indirect sex discrimination is prohibited with respect to "the scope of the schemes and the conditions of access thereto, the obligation to contribute and the calculation of contributions, the calculation of benefits including increases due in respect of a spouse and for dependants and the conditions governing the duration and retention of entitlements to benefits" (Article 4).

Member States have the right to exclude from the scope of Directive 79/7/EEC: (a) the pensionable age; (b) advantages granted to people who have brought up children; (c) old-age or invalidity benefit entitlement by virtue of the derived entitlements of a spouse; (d) the granting of increases in benefits for a dependent spouse in respect of long-term invalidity, old age, accidents at work and occupational disease; and (e) the consequences of exercising, before the adoption of the directive, a right of option not to acquire rights or incur obligations under a statutory scheme. The Member States are called upon to periodically examine whether it is justified to maintain the exclusions in the light of social developments (Article 7).

---

[61] See http://www.europarl.eu.int/comparl/libe/elsj/charter/art47/default_en.htm

Occupational pensions are regulated by *Council Directive 86/378/EEC of 24 July 1986 on the implementation of the principle of equal treatment for men and women in occupational social security schemes.* The directive applies to occupational schemes providing protection against the risks of sickness, invalidity, old age, industrial accidents, occupational diseases and unemployment. Subsequent to extensive case law of the European Court of Justice on occupational pensions, in which the Court applied Article 119 EEC rather than the directive, Council Directive 86/378/EEC was amended by *Council Directive 96/97/EC of 20 December 1996.*

Like Directive 79/7/EEC, Directive 86/378/EEC applies to the working population, including self-employed workers, workers whose activity is interrupted by illness, maternity, accident or involuntary unemployment, persons seeking employment, and retired and disabled workers (Article 3); the 1996 amendment extended the personal scope to those claiming under the insured persons in accordance with national law and/or practice. The material scope encompasses occupational schemes providing protection against the risks of sickness, invalidity, old age, industrial accidents, occupational diseases and unemployment, including occupational schemes which provide for other social benefits, such as survivors' benefits and family allowances if intended for employed persons (Article 4). Directive 86/378/EEC does not apply to individual contracts for self-employed workers, schemes for self-employed workers with only one member, insurance contracts not involving the employer, optional provisions of occupational schemes offered individually to participants, or occupational schemes financed by contributions paid by workers on a voluntary basis (Article 2).

The directive prohibits any discrimination based on sex, either directly or indirectly, making particular reference to marital or family status, especially as regards: (a) the scope of the schemes and the conditions of access to them; (b) the obligation to contribute and the calculation of the contributions; and (c) the calculation of benefits and the conditions governing the duration and retention of entitlement to benefits. The principle of equal treatment does not prejudice the provisions for the protection of women in respect of maternity (Article 5). In its original version, Article 9 of Directive 86/378/EEC permitted various distinctions based on sex. Most of these distinctions have been found to violate the principle of equal pay by the Court. Now, in its amended version, the directive takes up this case law and lists ten provisions based on sex that are contrary to the principle of equal treatment.

Provisions contrary to this principle which figure in legally compulsory collective agreements, staff rules of undertakings or any other arrangements must be declared null and void or amended. Any provisions of occupational schemes for employed workers contrary to the principle of equal treatment must be revised with retroactive effect from 17 May 1990, except in the case of workers who have, before that date, initiated legal proceedings. This is a consequence of the landmark *Barber* judgement (see Chapter 3).

Another directive in the field of social security, but one of little practical relevance, is *Council Directive 86/613/EEC of 11 December 1986 on the application of the principle of equal treatment between men and women engaged in an activity, including agriculture, in a self-employed capacity, and the protection of self-employed women during pregnancy and maternity.* The European Parliament recently called on the Member States to apply the equal opportunity principle in agricultural and rural development policies, particularly to support women farmers[62]. The Commission was requested to promote equal opportunities in the context of programmes and actions for rural development for the Member States. The European Parliament also asked the Commission to consider revising Council Directive 86/613/EEC, especially to make it more binding.

Council Directive 97/80/EC of 15 December 1997 on the burden of proof in cases of discrimination based on sex is of the utmost importance for judicial proceedings. It modifies the burden of proof in proceedings before any civil or administrative court or tribunal concerning the public or private sector. It was adopted as a reaction to important case law of the European Court of Justice on the burden of proof in the field of equal pay[63]. The scope of the directive extends to matters of equal treatment, maternity protection and parental leave (Article 3). The directive does not apply to criminal procedures, unless otherwise provided by the Member States. Application of Directives 79/7/EEC and 86/378/EEC is also excluded from its scope. Nevertheless, Directive 97/80/EC is relevant for occupational and state pensions, insofar as the equal pay principle is concerned. This latter aspect is most relevant in legal practice.

---

[62] *European Parliament Resolution on women in rural areas of the European Union in the light of the mid-term review of the common agricultural policy*, of 3 July 2003, see under: http://europa.eu.int/abc/doc/off/bull/en/200307/p103031.htm

[63] Case 109/88, *Handels- og Kontorfunktionærernes Forbund i Danmark v. Dansk Arbejdsgiverforening (Danfoss A/S)*, ECR 1989, p. 3199; Case C-127/92, *Enderby v. Frenchay Health Authority and Secretary of State for Health*, ECR 1993, p. I-5535. A summary of all rulings delivered by the European Court of Justice up to June 1998 in the field of sex equality is published in: *Handbook on equal treatment for women and men in the European Union*, 2nd edition, Office for Official Publications of the European Communities, 1999 (ISBN92-828-6662-9).

The case law mentioned above and Directive 97/80/EC have important consequences if an assertion is not proven. Normally, if a person files a legal complaint before a civil or labour court, it is up to her or him to prove the facts corresponding to the alleged claim. If the burden of proof is not met by the complainant, the opposing party does not need to defend the claim. The nature of discrimination cases, however, often makes it difficult or impossible for the complainant to provide the required evidence. In general, the complainant has little or no information on the employer's internal policies.

As of 1 January 2001, the implementation deadline of Directive 97/80/EC, the following is valid. When the plaintiff establishes facts on the basis of which discrimination may be presumed to exist, it is for the defendant to prove that there has been no contravention of the principle of equality. In other words, where a worker is able to show sufficient evidence for a case of discrimination (*prima facie* case), the burden of proof shifts to the employer. The employer must then rebut the evidence by showing legitimate reasons for a disadvantage suffered by the worker (Article 4). Article 2(2) defines the concept of indirect discrimination, in line with the case law of the European Court of Justice, as follows: "where an apparently neutral provision, criterion or practice disadvantages a substantially higher proportion of the members of one sex, unless that provision, criterion or practice is appropriate and necessary and can be justified by objective factors unrelated to sex." Through such a modification of the burden of proof, the information deficit on the side of the claimant is equalized, and he or she has a real chance of actually winning a discrimination case.

According to Article 3, Directive 97/80/EC applies to the situations covered by Article 141 EC and by Directive 75/117/EEC on equal pay, Directive 76/207/EEC on equal treatment, and, insofar as discrimination based on sex is concerned, Directive 92/85/EEC on maternity protection and Directive 96/34/EC on parental leave. It does not apply to situations falling under the scope of Directive 79/7/EEC on statutory social security and Directive 86/378/EEC on occupational social security. However, the Court tends to apply the principle of equal pay rather than the provisions on state and occupational pensions; and the modified procedure relating to the burden of proof is valid for matters of equal pay.

Directive 2000/78/EC of 27 November 2000 establishing a general framework for equal treatment in employment and occupation[64] should also be mentioned.

---

[64] See: http://europa.eu.int/comm/employment_social/fundamental_rights/publi/pubs_en.htm

This directive is primarily concerned with discrimination based on grounds other than sex. Its purpose is "to lay down a general framework for combating discrimination on the grounds of religion or belief, disability, age or sexual orientation as regards employment and occupation, with a view to putting into effect in the Member States the principle of equal treatment" (Article 1). Legislation and case law on sex equality have existed for decades. Directive 2000/78/EC, however, explicitly covers the protection of homosexual persons[65]. The Member States must have complied with the directive by 2 December 2003.

For financial services not connected with occupational or statutory pensions, sex may still be used as a determining factor for the calculation of premiums and benefits. In private insurance schemes, women often pay higher premiums for pensions and annuities, or the plans pay out less per year, while men pay higher premiums for life insurance or motor vehicle insurance. These differences are justified by the industry on the grounds that women live longer, or that men cause more – or more costly – accidents. At present, such a practice is not contrary to European law. In November 2003, the Commission presented a proposal for a directive to advance the principle of sex equality in the provision of goods and services[66]. This instrument would explicitly tackle premiums and benefits in the insurance sector. Sex neutrality in this field is a highly controversial issue. The proposal is based on Article 13 EC; its adoption requires unanimity in the Council. The likelihood of the proposal being adopted is thus questionable.

The following arguments have been put forward by the Commission. There are many factors that are not linked to sex but are equally important in establishing, for instance, life expectancy. These factors include socioeconomic or marital status, the region where a person lives, or lifestyle factors such as smoking and other hazardous habits. When these factors are removed from the calculations, differences in life expectancy purely on the grounds of sex are much less than currently stated. In health insurance, women are often charged higher premiums on the grounds that they might become pregnant and give birth, with the associated cost implications. In that situation, the discrimination arises from

---

[65] Under Directive 76/207/EEC, the European Court of Justice has employed the concept of sex equality for transsexual but not for homosexual persons. Concerning the latter, the Court pointed out that legislation could be adopted only on the basis of Article 13 EC, see Case C-13/94, *P v. S and Cornwall County Council*, ECR 1996, p. I-2143, and Case C-249/96, *Grant v. South-West Trains Ltd*, ECR 1998, p. I-621.

[66] See: http://europa.eu.int/rapid/start/cgi/guesten.ksh?p_action.gettxt=gt&doc=IP/03/1501|0|RAPID&lg=EN&display=

the fact that the whole of society benefits, whereas the costs are borne by one section of society alone.

Discussions are continuing on possible ways to improve the present legal system by simplifying the existing legislation in the area of equal treatment between men and women[67].

2.8 The Charter of Fundamental Rights of the European Union[68]

The *Charter of Fundamental Rights of the European Union* was solemnly proclaimed on 7 December 2000. The Charter does not introduce new individual rights, but the national courts are required to weigh limitations to the rights of equality, property and social security – all of which have to be considered in the context of social security entitlements – in view of the principles of legality and proportionality (Article 52)[69].

The Charter recognizes the following rights as fundamental. The right to property is granted in Article 17. Article 20 of the Charter states: "Everyone is equal before the law". Article 21 prohibits any discrimination on ground of "sex, race, colour, ethnic or social origin, genetic features, language, religion or belief, political or any other opinion, membership of a national minority, property, birth, disability, age or sexual orientation". The Union respects "cultural, religious and linguistic diversity" (Article 22). According to Article 23, "equality between men and women must be ensured in all areas, including employment, work and pay". Article 25 underlines "the rights of the elderly to lead a life of dignity and independence and to participate in social and cultural life". Article 26 stresses "the right of persons with disabilities to benefit from measures designed to ensure their independence, social and occupational integration and participation in the life of the community". In Article 34, the Union "recognises and respects the entitlement to social security benefits and social services providing protection in cases such as maternity, illness, industrial accidents, dependency or old age, and in the case of loss of employment, in accordance with the rules laid down by Community law and national laws and practices." And Article 47 confirms the right to an effective remedy and to a fair trial.

---

[67] See: http://europa.eu.int/comm/employment_social/news/2003/jul/options_en.pdf

[68] See: http://www.europarl.eu.int/comparl/libe/elsj/charter/default_en.htm

[69] See also footnote 58.

Chapter 3: Concepts of sex equality in various social security systems

3.1 Pay equality — A fundamental European right

Instruments to promote equality between men and women in the field of social security entail different concepts. Whereas the right to equal pay is to a large extent unconditional, the principle of equal treatment in social security schemes is limited in terms of personal and material scope. Directive 79/7/EEC on statutory schemes, as well as Directive 86/378/EEC in its original version, allows a number of sex-related derogations. The European Court of Justice has frequently looked at the different legal instruments and their respective consequences. Its interpretation of sex equality has promoted social justice and contributed to more effective protection against discrimination. In particular, the European Court of Justice has developed significant case law in the field of pay discrimination. The impact of that case law on social security matters is discussed below.

As early as 1976, in its landmark ruling on the *Defrenne II*[70] case, the Court declared pay equality a fundamental workers' right. Ms. Defrenne worked as a stewardess for the Belgian airline Sabena from 1951 to 1968. While she was employed, female stewardesses received a lower salary than male cabin stewards, although both groups did the same work. In 1968, her contract was terminated, because she had reached the age (40 years) at which women ceased to be members of the crew.

The legal background was the following: Article 119 EEC (now, after amendment, Article 141 EC) stated the right to equal pay regardless of sex. A transitional period of four years had elapsed, during which this right should have been implemented in all Founding States, but Belgium had failed to adopt legislation on equal pay. Forms of direct discrimination were not exceptional, but Ms. Defrenne insisted on equal treatment. She sued the Belgian State because the state pension she received after

---

[70] Case 43/75, *Defrenne v. Société Anonyme Belge de Navigation Aérienne Sabena,* ECR 1976, p. 455; for details see: I. Heide, "Supranational action against sex discrimination: Equal pay and equal treatment in the European Union", *International Labour Review,* Vol. 138, No. 4, 1999, pp. 381-410.

retirement was below her former income. From Sabena she claimed the difference in pay between her own income and that of the male stewards, as well as compensation for illegal dismissal. The Belgian court referred the three cases to the European Court of Justice for preliminary ruling.

The Court dismissed her first claim, since the right to equal pay is applicable only to payments made by the employer in connection with the employment, but not to statutory pension schemes. Such schemes are now covered by Directive 79/7/EEC, which had not been adopted at that time. The Court declared: "A retirement pension established within the framework of a social security scheme laid down by legislation does not constitute consideration which the worker receives indirectly in respect of his employment from his employer within the meaning of the second paragraph of Article 119 of the EEC Treaty"[71].

Ms. Defrenne's compensation claim for illegal dismissal was denied because the Equal Treatment Directive was not yet force[72]. The equal pay claim posed a similar problem, since during her employment the Equal Pay Directive was not in place either. So the question was whether Article 119 could serve as a direct basis for pay claims. It was also unclear how the "legal pay" could be determined when an employment contract was null and void because of a breach of equality law. Member States expressed great concern regarding the consequences of the ruling for all the other employees whose right to equal pay had been violated.

On 8 April 1976, a historic date for sex equality, the Court delivered its groundbreaking ruling. It held that Article 119 EEC, because of its "distinct and fundamental" character, had "direct vertical and horizontal effects" and could be invoked for individual claims of equal pay made against any private or public employer. The Court stressed the Community task of improving living and working conditions, and concluded that the person discriminated against must be treated exactly like the comparative group. This meant a levelling up of rights until new legal rules that applied the equality principle correctly were in place. Ms. Defrenne was thus entitled to receive pay at the level of the male stewards from 1 January 1962, when the Article entered into effect, until her dismissal in 1968. But because of "overriding considerations of legal

---

[71] Case 80/70, *Defrenne v. Belgian State (Defrenne I)*, ECR 1971, p. 445. For recent case law on pensions in the public service see Chapter 3.6.

[72] Case 149/77, *Defrenne v. Société Anonyme Belge de Navigation Aérienne Sabena (Defrenne III)*, ECR 1978, p. 1365.

certainty", the entitlement was limited by the Court to this and other cases pending. All other employees who have been discriminated against are entitled to equal pay from the day of this ruling, 8 April 1976. New Member States must abide by the principle of equal pay as from the day of accession.

3.2 Equal pay and occupational pensions: Bilka, Barber and post-Barber

Article 7 of Directive 79/7/EEC on statutory pension schemes allows Member States to maintain certain distinctions based on sex with respect to: the retirement age; advantages for people who have brought up children; old-age and invalidity benefits for spouses; and the granting of increases in cases of long-term invalidity, accidents at work and occupational disease benefits for a dependent spouse. A similar provision was included for occupational schemes in the original Article 9 of Directive 86/378/EEC. In contrast, where Article 141 (ex-Article 119) applies, it supersedes the limited concept of equal treatment laid down in the above-mentioned provisions and permits no deviation from the principle of equality.

The equal pay principle prohibits any distinction to be made between men and women (direct discrimination), and any practice that has a negative effect for the majority of the workers of one sex unless such a practice can be justified by entirely neutral factors (indirect discrimination). The effect of the principle of equal pay in the context of different contributions made by the employer for male and female employees was first decided in 1981. In *Worringham and Humphreys v. Lloyd's Bank Ltd*[73], the employer made an additional contribution of 5% for male employees only to an occupational pension scheme. The question was whether such a distinction based on sex was compatible with European law.

The European Court of Justice, to which this question was referred, made it clear that contributions paid by an employer in the name of employees by means of an addition to the gross salary were "pay" within the meaning of Article 119 EEC. It concluded that the national courts "have a duty to ensure the protection of the rights which this provision vests

---

[73] Case 69/80, ECR 1981, p. 767.

in individuals, in particular in a case where, because of the requirement imposed only on men or only on women to contribute to a retirement benefits scheme, the contributions in question are paid by the employer in the name of the employee and deducted from the gross salary whose amount they determine".

A related matter concerning obligatory contribution to a survivors' fund was dealt with in Case 192/85[74]. Mr. Newstead, a civil servant and confirmed bachelor, belonged to an occupational pension scheme that made provision for a widows' pension fund. This fund was financed in part by the contributions of civil servants, but only the men were obliged to contribute. The contribution took the form of a deduction of 1.5% from the gross salary of the male civil servants. The men therefore received lower net pay than the female civil servants. The obligatory contribution was regarded as compatible with the equality principle, because the gross salary paid to the male and female staff was the same. The Court stressed that Article 1(2) of Directive 76/207/EEC on equal treatment excluded from its scope matters of social security for which specific legislation was to be adopted. The subsequent Directive 79/7/EEC did not apply to survivors' pensions, and Directive 86/378/EEC on occupational pension schemes allowed Member States to "defer compulsory application of the principle of equal treatment with regard to: ... (b) survivors' pensions until a directive requires the principle of equal treatment in statutory social security schemes in that regard". Today, in view of the recent case law on pensions in the public service (described below) and Articles 2 and 6(1)(i) as amended by Directive 96/97/EC, such a practice would probably be considered illegal.

According to the Court's case law, all pension schemes must be regarded first and foremost under the aspect of equal pay. The principles of equal pay and equal treatment at the workplace, covered by Article 141 EC (ex-Article 119 EEC) and the Directives 75/117/EEC and 76/207/EEC, have been interpreted widely, as requiring absolute equality between the sexes. Directives 79/7/EEC and 86/378/EEC – the latter in its original version – have been construed restrictively insofar as they permit distinctions from the principle of equality. The equal pay principle, as defined in *Defrenne II*, is of particular interest for employees who have worked since the mid-1970s and are now reaching pensionable age; where the right to equal pay has been violated, the victim is entitled to retroactive contributions as from 8 April 1976, the day of the ruling. For

---

[74] *Newstead v. Department of Transport and Her Majesty's Treasury*, ECR 1987, p. 4753.

the accession countries, the date of accession is decisive. Based on the Court's ruling, the concept of direct and indirect discrimination in occupational pension schemes was later defined in the famous *Bilka*[75], *Barber* and *post-Barber* cases[76].

In *Bilka*, the question brought before the Court was whether the exclusion of part-time workers from membership in an occupational pension scheme amounts to indirect discrimination if such exclusion affects disproportionately more women than men. The Court agreed with the claimant that this was the case and declared:

> Article 119 of the EEC Treaty is infringed by a department store company which excludes part-time employees from its occupational pension scheme, where that exclusion affects a far greater number of women than men, unless the undertaking shows that the exclusion is based on objectively justified factors unrelated to any discrimination on grounds of sex.

The excluded claimant, Ms. Weber von Hartz, was entitled to retroactive consideration of benefits as from 8 April 1976, the date of the *Defrenne II* judgement.

The *Barber* and numerous *post-Barber* cases have posed a variety of problems in the context of pensionable ages. Different pensionable ages for men and women are legitimate in statutory pension schemes. The same was valid for occupational pensions under Directive 86/378/EEC in its original version. It was obviously in good faith that many employer-financed pension schemes, especially those replacing state pensions, reflected the same differentiation. This widespread practice disadvantaged men who were members of such schemes because they were entitled to the pension at a higher age than women members.

Mr. Barber was a member of a contracted-out pension scheme, a substitute for the state pension scheme, approved under the United Kingdom Social Security Act of 1975. In the event of redundancy, male members of the fund were entitled to an immediate pension at the age of 55 years, females at the age of 50 years. Mr. Barber was dismissed for organizational reasons at the age of 52. His pension was deferred; had he been a female employee of 52, he would have been treated as

---

[75] Case 170/84, *Bilka-Kaufhaus GmbH v. Weber von Hartz*, ECR 1986, p. 1607. See also footnote 70 and the judgement of 13 January 2004 on Case C-256/01, *Allonby v. Accrington & Rossendale College*, http://www.curia.eu.int/jurisp/cgi-bin...6&doc=T&ouvert=T&seance=ARRET&where=().

[76] Case 262/88, *Barber v. Guardian Royal Exchange Assurance Group*, ECR 1990, p. I-1889; Case C-110/91, *Moroni v. Collo GmbH*, ECR 1993, p. I-6591; Case C-152/91, *Neath v. Steeper Ltd*, ECR 1993, p. I-6935; Case C-200/91, *Coloroll Pension Trustees Limited v. Russel and Others*, ECR 1994, p. I-4389; C-408/92, *Smith and Others v. Avdel Systems Ltd*, ECR 1994, p. I-4435.

having retired and would have been entitled to an immediate pension. He took the view that he was a victim of unlawful discrimination based on sex.

The European Court of Justice agreed with Mr. Barber. It found that the occupational pension fell within the scope of equal pay, although it replaced the state pension scheme. Discrimination between men and women is prohibited not only when the age of entitlement to an occupational pension is established, but also when the pension is offered by way of compensation for dismissal on economic grounds. In view of the Articles 7(1) of Directive 79/7/EEC and 9(a) of Directive 86/378/EEC, however, such a ruling was hardly to be expected. As in *Defrenne II*, the Court limited retroactive entitlement to the pending cases. It acknowledged that the parties concerned were reasonably entitled to consider that Article 119 did not apply, and that derogations from the principle of equality between men and women with respect to the pensionable age were permitted. In order to safeguard the financial balance of the schemes in question, the retroactive effect resulting from *Defrenne II* was limited to cases pending. Other claimants in the same situation have rights as from 17 May 1990, the day of the *Barber* ruling. In its later judgements on "purely" private occupational pension schemes[77], the Court reiterated the right to equal pay from the same date.

The Maastricht Treaty provided for a number of changes, including on social matters. The Member States, concerned about more far-reaching retroactive claims, confirmed the *Barber* deadline in the *Protocol on Article 119 of the Treaty establishing the European Community*. The so-called Barber Protocol was annexed to the Treaty and reads as follows:

> For the purposes of Article 119 of this Treaty, benefits under occupational social security schemes shall not be considered as remuneration if and in so far as they are attributable to periods of employment prior to 17 May 1990, except in the case of workers or those claiming under them who have before that date initiated legal proceedings or introduced an equivalent claim under the applicable national law.

The same deadline was applied in *Defreyn v. Sabena SA*[78] on an additional early retirement pension granted to men and women at different ages.

The validity of time limits for retroactive pay has important financial implications for the social partners. The Barber ruling enforced retro-

---

[77] Case C-109/91, *Ten Oever v. Stichting Bedrijfspensioenfonds voor het Glazenwassers-En Schoonmaakbedrijf*, ECR 1993, p. I-4879; Case C-110/91, *Moroni v. Collo GmbH*, ECR 1993, p. I-6591.

[78] Case C-166/99, ECR 2000, p. I-6155.

active consideration for occupational pensions only from May 1990 and not, as in the *Defrenne II* and *Bilka* cases, from April 1976. The higher level of benefit must be granted to the disadvantaged group (levelling up) until men and women are treated equally on a new legal basis, for instance by a superseding collective agreement. This cannot be done retroactively. The way in which the 14 years between 1976 and 1990 – and possibly even before 1976 – are considered obviously has important consequences for both workers and employers. This is why further cases were submitted to the Court for preliminary ruling on the different possible time limits.

Five former employees of the German postal and telecommunication services demanded retroactive consideration of employment periods in the 1960s and 1970s. Ms. Vick and Ms. Conze were employed by Versorgungsanstalt der Deutschen Bundespost (VAP), which was later succeeded by Deutsche Telekom[79]. During 1971 and 1972, they worked on a part-time basis below the minimum threshold of 18 hours. Ms. Vick's former membership of the pension scheme was terminated and her part of the contributions reimbursed. Ms. Conze was affiliated until 1972 and, after amendment of the collective pensions agreement with effect from April 1991, re-affiliated from this date. Ms. Schröder was employed part-time from 1974 until 1994, while Ms. Sievers and Ms. Schrage were employed part-time between 1960 and 1988. According to the *Bilka* ruling, they would have been entitled to retroactive consideration as from 8 April 1976, the day of the *Defrenne II* ruling. They claimed that their exclusion from occupational pension schemes was linked with part-time employment; it constituted discrimination based on sex and also discrimination against part-time workers. They relied on the date of the *Defrenne II* judgement and on national case law on compensation for part-time workers who had been discriminated against, which set no time limit for retroactive rights.

The exclusion of part-time workers working less than a specified number of hours from a company pension affected 95% of the female staff and was not objectively justified. All parties recognized that the practice constituted indirect discrimination on the grounds of sex. The disputed question was which period had to be considered for the calculation of benefits. Deutsche Telekom submitted that the rights claimed could at best be upheld from 17 May 1990, the date of the *Barber* judgement.

---

[79] Joined Cases C-234/96 and C-235/96, *Vick and Conze v. Deutsche Telekom AG*, ECR 2000, p. I-799; Joined Cases C-270/97 and C-271/97, *Sievers and Schrage v. Deutsche Post*, ECR 2000, p. I-929 and p. I-920; C-50/96, *Schröder v. Deutsche Telekom AG*, ECR 2000, p. I-743.

A further problem was that the exclusion of part-time workers from a company pension scheme also constituted unlawful discrimination against part-time workers, whose compensation had no time limit under domestic law.

The questions brought before the European Court of Justice were the following. Could the Barber Protocol limit the rights based on national law prohibiting discrimination against part-time workers? Was the national court under an obligation to decline to apply the more favourable treatment prescribed by national law? Would more favourable treatment of workers in one Member State lead to unlawful distortion of competition within the Community, which Article 141 EC was aimed to prevent?

The Court denied the validity of the limitations in time of the Barber judgement and Protocol with respect of the right to join an occupational pension scheme and to entitlements from such a scheme. Part-time workers who are unlawfully excluded from membership of an occupational pension scheme can normally claim retroactive compensation as from 8 April 1976, the date of the *Defrenne II* ruling. However, this ruling does not preclude more favourable treatment under national law. The Court concluded that national law may grant further rights to prohibit discrimination against part-time workers as such, irrespective of their sex.

The Court acknowledged that this interpretation might disadvantage the companies residing in Germany, but it considered the social aim of Article 141 EC (to realize the principle of equal pay) as prior over its economic aim (to prevent distortion of competition). The claimants who had been working part-time in the 1960s and early 1970s and had unlawfully been excluded from the employer-financed pension scheme had therefore accrued entitlements during their entire employment. The Court also pointed out that the right to claim retroactive membership of a scheme did not enable the claimant to avoid paying contributions for the period of membership concerned, if that was required under the scheme. Those who had been reimbursed for their part of the contributions were therefore required to pay that amount back.

The date of the *Defrenne II* ruling was also applied in the case *Dietz v. Stichting Thuiszorg Rotterdam*[80]. The case dealt with a scheme which

---

[80] Case C-435/93, ECR 1996, p. I-5223; see also Case C- 28/93, *Van den Akker and Others v. Stichting Shell Pensioenfonds*, ECR 1994, p. I-4527.

excluded part-time workers who worked less than 40% of the ordinary working hours; membership of the scheme was declared compulsory by the Dutch Government. In a similar case, *Magorrian and Cunningham*[81], an additional problem was whether the entitlement could be limited by virtue of national law to a period of two years prior to the commencement of proceedings in connection with the claim. The Court found such a limitation not justified.

The following can be concluded on the basis of the Court's rulings. Part-time workers who have been unlawfully excluded from membership of an occupational pension scheme are entitled to benefits as from 8 April 1976 (the judgement on *Defrenne II*) or from the day of the country's accession to the Community. If national law permits consideration of periods before that date, the more favourable provisions apply, even if this might cause a competitive disadvantage for the companies residing in the country concerned. The same is valid for cases pending before 8 April 1976. The time limit of the *Barber* judgement and of the Protocol (17 May 1990) applies to occupational pensions where a different pensionable age was fixed for women and men, unless the case was pending before that date. It is irrelevant whether the scheme in question replaces the state pension scheme, whether it is managed by the employer or any private trust or agency, whether it is paid on a pay-as-you-go basis, and whether membership is mandatory or not.

The case of *Boyle and Others v. Equal Opportunities Commission*[82] is noteworthy with respect to occupational pension entitlements acquired during maternity leave. The maintenance of labour law rights in the context of pregnancy and maternity is covered by the Equal Treatment Directive 76/207/EEC and by *Directive 92/85/EEC of 19 October 1992 on the introduction of measures to encourage improvements in the safety and health at work of pregnant workers and workers who have recently given birth or are breastfeeding.* The maternity scheme applicable – which formed part of each employment contract – limited the accrual of pension rights to periods during maternity leave in which the woman receives pay, and not sickness maintenance payment (SMP). A woman who fell ill during maternity leave was therefore excluded from entitlement. Is such a policy in compliance with Articles 8(1) and 11(2)(a) of Directive 92/85/EC

---

[81] Case C-246/96, *Magorrian and Cunningham v. Eastern Health and Social Services Board and Department of Health and Social Services*, ECR 1997, p. I-7153; see also Case C-57/93, *Vroege v. NCIV Instituut voor Volkshuisvesting BV and Stichting Pensioenfonds NCIV*, ECR 1994, p. I-4541 and Case C-128/93, *Fisscher v. Voorhuis Hengelo BV and Stichting Bedrijfspensioenfonds voor de Detailhandel*, ECR 1994, p. I- 4583.

[82] Case C-411/96, ECR 1998, p. I-6401.

which guarantees the maintenance of employment rights during the pre-scribed minimum of 14 weeks maternity leave?

The Court pointed out that the employer has the duty to maintain all employment rights during the period of maternity leave including the women's right to continued pay. Directive 92/85/EEC therefore

> precludes a clause in an employment contract from limiting, in the con-text of an occupational scheme wholly financed by the employer, the accrual of pension rights during the period of maternity leave referred to by Article 8 of that directive to the period during which the woman receives the pay provided for by that contract or national legislation.

Although an employment contract may provide for a period of supple-mentary unpaid maternity leave, it cannot, without infringing Community law, limit the period during which pensions rights accrue to the period of paid leave.

Hungary and Poland have introduced mixed pension schemes, under which part of each worker's monthly pension contribution is redirected to a commercially managed individual savings account. At retirement, the savings accumulated are converted to an annuity that will pay a monthly pension benefit until the worker's death[83]. The new private old-age insurance is an addition to the state pension scheme, mandatory for all workers and managed commercially as individual savings accounts. It is meant to replace a portion of the public pay-as-you-go schemes in those countries. Part of the workers' contributions are placed as savings with private investors. The reforms were undertaken in the context of the privatization of state enterprises in the former socialist systems, and in order to boost private markets. The benefits are aimed at providing a second pillar of monthly payments after retirement, additional to the state pension.

If payments from these individual savings accounts are calculated sepa-rately for women and men, taking into consideration the longer life expectancy of women, is this a lawful distinction between the sexes or unlawful sex discrimination? Such an approach would lower the monthly payments made to female old-age pensioners. Its legality under European law is questionable, since the contributions made by the employees are an element of their salary, and the pensions result from the employment relationship. Thus, no distinction based on sex should

---

[83] See footnote 11, p. 16 and 36 et seq.

be made with regard to the benefits granted to male and female members of such a private scheme.

In one of its rulings[84], the Court accepted the use of actuarial factors differing according to sex, but only in relation to the funding of a defined-benefit scheme. It stressed that the employer's commitment concerns the payment, at a given moment, of a periodic pension for which the determining criteria are already known at the time when the commitment is made. A separate question concerned the choice of funding arrangements to secure the fund's assets. In the view of the Court, the funding arrangements enable the employer to meet the obligations connected with the scheme. They are relevant for the relationship between the fund and the employer, but have no direct impact on the benefit as such. As long as the benefits paid to male and female pensioners are the same, the employer is free to choose any suitable form of investment. Such a decision does not fall under the scope of Article 141 EC or Directive 75/117/EEC.

Neath v. Steeper has been taken up in the wording of Directive 86/378/EEC, as revised by Directive 96/97/EC. Its new Article 6(h) prohibits the setting of different levels of benefit in the case of defined-contribution schemes. It further states: "In the case of funded defined-benefit schemes, certain elements ... may be unequal where the inequality of the amounts results from the effects of the use of actuarial factors differing according to sex at the time when the scheme's funding is implemented."

3.3 Equal conditions for survivors' pensions in occupational schemes

Directive 86/378/EEC is applicable to "occupational schemes which provide for other social benefits, in cash or in kind, and in particular survivors' benefits and family allowances, if such benefits are accorded to employed persons and thus constitute a consideration paid by the employer to the worker by reason of the latter's employment" (Article 4(b)). In contrast to Directive 79/7/EEC, it covers not only the risks of old age, early retirement or invalidity, but also an insurance for the surviving husband or wife of the employee.

---

[84] Case C-152/91, *Neath v. Hugh Steeper Ltd*, ECR 1993, p. I-6935.

As a result of the traditional understanding of the roles of men and women in society, in particular that of the male as the breadwinner of the family, survivors' benefits are not always granted under the same conditions to widows and widowers. Article 9(b) of Directive 86/378/EEC originally allowed Member States to defer compulsory application with regard to survivors' pensions. But distinctions that are made for male and female survivors may also violate the principle of equal pay. On various occasions, the Court was requested to judge whether or not such benefits are received by the worker from the employer, if paid by a legally independent trustee or insurance agent.

Ms. Evrenopoulos had worked for the Greek state electricity company, Dimossia Epicheirissi Ilektrismou (DEI). DEI is a state body *sui generis*, acting as employer under private law. The DEI insurance scheme covered pensions, health insurance and welfare assistance and was exclusively regulated by legislation. All persons employed, together with members of their families, were compulsorily subject to that scheme. The law provided that "in the event of the death of the pensioner... the widow, or, where the person insured was a widower − if he is without means and totally unfit for work and was maintained by the deceased throughout the five years preceding her death − is entitled to a pension." Mr. Evrenopoulos[85] who was not "without means and totally unfit for work" claimed a survivor's pension following his wife's death, which was denied by the fund.

The Court pointed out that pensions paid under statutory social security schemes might reflect, wholly or in part, pay in respect of work. In such schemes, considerations of social policy, state organization and ethics, or even budgetary concerns might influence the establishment by the national legislature of a particular scheme. Considerations of social policy could not prevail if the pension concerned only a particular category of workers, if it was directly related to length of service and if its amount was calculated by reference to the last salary. The DEI's survivors' pension essentially arose from the employment of the beneficiary's spouse. It was linked to her pay and clearly fell within the scope of Article 119 of the EEC Treaty. Since Mr. Evrenopoulos had instituted proceedings before 17 May 1990, the date of the *Barber* ruling, he was entitled to the pension from January 1989[86].

---

[85] Case C-147/95, *Dimossia Epicheirissi Ilektrismou (DEI) v. Evrenopoulos*, ECR 1997, p. I-2057.

[86] For failure to transpose Directive 96/97/EC amending Directive 86/378/EEC, see Case C-457/98, *Commission of the European Communities v. Hellenic Republic*, ECR 2000, p. I-11481.

Ms. Podesta worked as a senior executive in the French pharmaceutical industry. For 35 years, she had paid contributions in respect of a supplementary retirement pension. The legal basis was a collective agreement which made provision for a survivor's benefit from the age of 60 years for the widow of a member or from the age of 65 years for a widower. Following her death in 1993, the surviving husband applied for a pension which was half of the retirement pension due to his wife. He was refused on the ground that he had not yet reached the age of 65, the age prescribed for widowers. Mr. Podesta[87] claimed that the provisions under which the male survivors must have reached the age of 65, whereas the age fixed for female survivors was 60, were in breach of the principle of equal pay for men and women. The French *Tribunal de Grande Instance* put forward the question of whether or not Article 119 EEC precluded discrimination between men and women in respect of the age at which their spouses were entitled to a survivor's pension.

The pension fund contended that the supplementary retirement pension scheme in question was an inter-occupational pay-as-you-go scheme, which was compulsory for all employees. It met considerations of social policy but not those of a particular occupation, and was therefore justified by legitimate aims of social policy. This view was not shared by the Court, which upheld the ruling that the only decisive criterion was whether or not the pension was paid by reason of the employment relationship. A survivor's pension provided for by an occupational pension scheme was an advantage deriving from the survivor's spouse's membership of the scheme and accordingly fell within the scope of equal pay. The scheme in question was not designed for the whole population or all workers. The fact that the national legislature extended the applicability of occupational schemes to various categories of employees was not sufficient to take those schemes outside the scope of equal pay, if it was established that the schemes were intended in principle for current or former employees of the undertakings concerned.

The Court examined the material scope of Directive 86/378/EEC, as amended by Directive 96/97/EC. Article 2(1) defines "occupational social security schemes" as

> schemes not governed by Directive 79/7/EEC whose purpose is to provide workers, whether employees or self-employed, in an undertaking or group of undertakings, area of economic activity, occupational sector

---

[87] Case C-50/99, *Podesta v. Caisse de retraite par répartition des ingénieurs cadres & assimilés (CRICA) and Others,* ECR 2000, p. I-4039.

or group of sectors with benefits intended to supplement the benefits provided by statutory social security schemes or to replace them, whether
membership of such schemes is compulsory or optional.

The Court concluded that the fact that membership of the occupational
social security scheme was compulsory was perfectly in line with this
definition and did not require another judgement.

Mr. Menauer[88] challenged the validity of a similar clause applicable to
his deceased wife's occupational pension fund. She was employed by
the Barmer Private Sickness Insurance Fund from 1956 until her death
in November 1993. The Fund's collective agreement granted a survivor's
pension to widowers only "where the deceased was the main breadwinner in the family".

The Court recalled that a retirement pension paid under an occupational
scheme set up under a collective agreement constituted "pay", no matter whether it replaced a statutory scheme or was supplementary to it.
According to the Court's ruling, the fact that such a pension is not paid
to the employee but to her surviving husband does not affect that interpretation. The pension is vested in and paid to the survivor by reason
of the employment relationship between the employer and the survivor's
spouse. This obligation extends to an independent body, such as a
German pension fund, since:

> the effectiveness of Article 119 of the Treaty would be considerably dimin-
> ished and the legal protection required to ensure real equality would be
> seriously impaired if an employee or an employee's dependants could rely
> on that provision only as against the employer, and not as against those
> who are expressly charged with performing the employer's obligations.

The pension funds entrusted with administering occupational pension
schemes are bound by the principle of equal pay in the same way as the
employer, and neither the legal independence that the funds enjoy nor
their status as insuring bodies are relevant.

It can thus be concluded that survivors' benefits deriving from an occupational pension scheme must be paid under equal conditions to widows and widowers. This is valid for any pension fund, as long as the entitlement results from an employment relationship and is based on a
collective agreement or other type of contract. It is irrelevant how such

---

[88] Case C-379/99, *Menauer v. Pensionskasse für die Angestellten der Barmer Ersatzkasse VVaG*, ECR 2001,
p. I-7275.

funds are organized and whether they are fully private, inter-occupational, or supplementary to the state pension scheme, and how – particularly in which legal form – or by whom they are managed.

3.4 The principle of equal treatment in statutory pension schemes (Directive 79/7/EEC)

Directive 79/7/EEC specifically deals with social security benefits that are governed by statute and apply compulsorily to general categories of workers. In principle, it prohibits both direct and indirect discrimination, in particular through reference to marital or family status. It nevertheless allows specified derogations at the national level. The directive seeks to implement the principle of equal treatment in the statutory schemes that provide protection against the risks of sickness, invalidity, old age, accidents at work, occupational diseases and unemployment, as well as the social assistance schemes that are intended to supplement or replace those statutory schemes. Thus the aim of the directive is the progressive elimination of discrimination between the sexes in the social security systems of the Member States in terms of payments to those who are unable to continue in paid work for one of the stated reasons. Some basic elements of the Court's interpretation of the directive are outlined in sections 3.4.1 to 3.4.5 below.

3.4.1 Personal scope: The "working population" (Article 2)

Article 2 states: "This Directive shall apply to the working population – including self-employed persons, workers and self-employed persons whose activity is interrupted by illness, accident or involuntary unemployment and persons seeking employment – and to retired or invalided workers and self-employed persons." Like Article 141 EC and Directives 75/117/EEC and 76/207/EEC, it is valid for persons who work in the EU Member States and in the three EFTA States Iceland, Liechtenstein and Norway[89].

---

[89] For Norway's policy on reservation of academic positions for women see EFTA Court of Justice on Case E-1/02, *EFTA Surveillance Authority v. Norway*, http://www.eftacourt.lu/pdf/01-02AdvisoryOpinion-E.pdf

Directive 79/7/EEC does not apply to persons who have never had an occupation and are not seeking work, nor to persons who have had an occupation that was interrupted but not by one of the risks referred to in Article 3(1)(a) and who are not seeking work[90]. A person who interrupts her or his occupational activity in order to raise a child and who is prevented from returning to employment by illness is not covered by the directive, "unless that person was seeking employment and his or her search was interrupted by the materialisation of one of the risks specified in Article 3(1)(a)"[91]. A non-employed person falls under the scope of this directive, when the reasons why he or she gave up employment arise from the risks mentioned in Article 3. Such a case was that of Ms. Drake.

Ms. Drake[92] was married and lived with her husband. She held a variety of full-time and part-time jobs until 1984. Then her mother, who received an attendance allowance under the United Kingdom Social Security Act, came to live with her. Ms. Drake gave up her job to look after her mother and applied for an invalid care allowance under the same Act. She was told that married women who lived with their husbands were not entitled to the allowance, in contrast to married men in the same situation. The underlying perception obviously was that a woman living with her husband should perform unpaid care work without any consideration under the social security scheme. The questions brought before the European Court of Justice were whether the risk of invalidity in the person of Ms. Drake's mother was covered by Directive 79/7/EEC, and whether Ms. Drake herself, who had given up her work and was not seeking employment, fell under its personal scope.

The Court defined the term "working population" broadly to include a person whose work had been interrupted by one of the risks referred to in Article 3. Although the insured worker and the invalid person were not identical, the Court argued that the requested allowance was part of a statutory scheme providing protection against one of the specified risks or a form of social assistance. Under such circumstances, the principle of equality must be extended to the person delivering the care. With

---

[90] Joined Cases 48/88, 106/88 and 107/88, *Achterberg-Te Riele and Others v. Sociale Verzekeringsbank Amsterdam*, ECR 1989, p. 1963.

[91] Case C-31/90, *Johnson v. Chief Adjudication Officer*, ECR 1991, p. I-3723.

[92] Case 150/85, *Drake v. Chief Adjudication Officer*, ECR 1986, p. 1995; see also Case C-165/91, *Van Munster v. Rijksdienst voor Pensioenen*, ECR 1994, p. I-4661, on a "household rate" for a worker's spouse who has ceased all gainful employment and is not in receipt of a retirement pension or an equivalent benefit.

respect to the negative condition imposed on women only, the Court decided that:

> discrimination on grounds of sex contrary to Article 4(1) of the Directive 79/7/EEC arises where legislation provides that a benefit which forms part of one of the statutory schemes referred to in Article 3(1) of that Directive is not payable to a married woman who lives with or is maintained by her husband, although it is paid in corresponding circumstances to a married man.

This ruling clearly fostered the social protection of women who fulfil unpaid tasks of family care.

3.4.2 Material scope: Statutory schemes and substituting social assistance benefits (Article 3)

Article 3 (1) of Directive 79/7/EEC defines the material scope of the directive as follows:

> (a) statutory schemes which provide protection against the following risks: sickness, invalidity, old age, accidents at work and occupational diseases, unemployment; (b) social assistance, in so far as it is intended to supplement or replace the schemes referred to in (a).

The risks covered under state pension schemes are clearly defined, but it often is unclear whether social assistance benefits are a supplement or replacement of them. Such questions have been raised in connection with income support, housing benefit and concessionary fares for low-income groups.

According to the United Kingdom Social Security Act of 1986, a housing benefit was payable to persons whose real income was lower than a notional income known as the "applicable amount". The housing benefit was determined, *inter alia,* by a "higher pensioner premium" paid to persons aged between 60 and 80 years, who lived alone and were in receipt of one or more other social security benefits, including an invalidity pension. The invalidity pension was payable up to the pensionable age, which was 60 years for women and 65 years for men. As a consequence of the applicable rules Ms. Smithson[93] did not receive the housing benefit between the ages of 60 and 65 and felt that she was discriminated against.

---

[93] Case C-243/90, *The Queen v. Secretary of State for Social Security, ex-parte Smithson,* ECR 1992, p. I-467.

The Court ruled that such a housing benefit was not covered by Directive 79/7/EEC. In order to fall within its scope, a benefit should "constitute the whole or part of a statutory scheme providing protection against one of the specified risks or a form of social assistance having the same objective". In order to be so identified the benefit should be "directly and effectively linked to the protection provided against one of the risks specified in Article 3(1) of the Directive". The respective provision did not refer to statutory schemes that were intended to guarantee a special allowance for housing costs to any person whose real income was lower than a notional income, calculated on the basis of certain criteria. The age and invalidity of the beneficiary were only two of the criteria applied in order to determine the beneficiary's financial need for such an allowance. The fact that these criteria were decisive as regards eligibility for the higher pensioner premium was not sufficient to bring that benefit within the scope of Directive 79/7/EEC.

In *Jackson and Cresswell v. Chief Adjudication Officer*[94], the Court looked at supplementary income support paid under the United Kingdom Supplementary Benefits Act of 1986. This benefit was awarded under a variety of circumstances to persons whose means were insufficient to meet their needs. The claimants were exempt from the obligation to be available for work. Ms. Jackson and Ms. Cresswell claimed that child-minding expenses incurred during periods of training or part-time employment must be deductible from the mother's income in order to avoid indirect discrimination. The Court did not share their view. It regarded the benefit as not directly and effectively linked to protection against the risk of unemployment, because the supplementary income benefit was paid even when the recipients were not available for work.

The granting of concessionary fares on public transport services to old-age pensioners and young or disabled persons was questioned in the case of Mr. Atkins[95]. At the age of 63 years, he was refused public transport travel concessions in his district, whereas a woman of the same age would have been entitled to such concessions. The challenged scheme applied to people with disabilities and to male old-age pensioners over the age of 65 years and female old-age pensioners over the age of 60 years. The Court pointed out that the aim of concessionary fares was to facilitate access to public transport for certain classes of persons who are recognized as having a particular need for transport and who are less

---

[94] Cases C-63/91 and C-64/91, ECR 1992, p. I-4737; see also *Meyers v. Adjudication Officer*, footnote 121.
[95] Case C-228/94, *Atkins v. Wrekin District Council and Department of Transport*, ECR 1996, p. I-3633.

well off financially. Such a benefit did not afford direct and effective protection against one of the risks listed in Article 3(1). Social assistance is covered by Directive 79/7/EEC only where it is intended to supplement or replace the schemes referred to in that provision – a condition which was not fulfilled by the concessionary fares.

3.4.3   The principle of equal treatment and its direct effects (Article 4)

Article 5 of Directive 79/7/EEC imposes on Member States the obligation to take "the measures necessary to ensure that any laws, regulations and administrative provisions contrary to the principle of equal treatment are abolished". According to Article 6, they are obliged to "introduce into their national legal systems such measures as are necessary to enable all persons who consider themselves wronged by failure to apply the principle of equal treatment to pursue their claims by judicial process, possibly after recourse to other competent authorities." Despite a long implementation period of six years, some Member States did not amend national law accordingly, and the consequences of such failure were soon brought before the courts.

The grant of an unemployment benefit was at stake in *The Netherlands v. Federatie Nederlandse Vakbeweging*[96]. In the Netherlands, a legal provision excluded from the right to unemployment benefit married women "who were not regarded as breadwinners and who did not live permanently separated from their husbands". Such a derogation from the principle of equality is not allowed by the directive. The Dutch Government, in an effort to transpose the directive, had proposed an amendment to the Law on Unemployment Benefit, but the Bill was rejected in Parliament. The matter was referred to the Court for preliminary ruling as to whether the disputed provision was still applicable after 23 December 1984 (the deadline for transposal), and what benefits the excluded women could claim.

The Court pointed out that, taken by itself and in the light of the objective and content of Directive 79/7/EEC, Article 4(1) was sufficiently precise to be relied upon by an individual and applied by the courts, and that women must be granted the same benefits as men:

---

[96] Case 71/85, ECR 1986, p. 3855.

> Where no measures have been adopted to implement Council Directive 79/7/EEC of 19 December 1978, Article 4(1) thereof, which prohibits all discrimination on grounds of sex in matters of social security, could be relied on as from 23 December 1984 in order to preclude the application of any national provision inconsistent with that article. In the absence of measures implementing that article, women are entitled to be treated in the same manner, and to have the same rules applied to them, as men who are in the same situation, since, where the Directive has not been implemented, those rules remain the only valid point of reference.

The same law in an amended version was under scrutiny in Case 80/87[97]. It included a transitional provision on the basis of which a married woman who had become unemployed before 23 December 1984 remained subject even after that date to the requirement that she be a wage-earner. The amendment was adopted after expiry of the period prescribed by the directive. The Court pointed out that Directive 79/7/EEC did not confer on Member States the discretion to uphold the former distinction based on sex for a transitional period. The law was declared contrary to the directive; the claimants were entitled to the same benefits as men, without having to prove that they were the family breadwinner.

A similar case concerned unemployment benefit that was limited in time for married women only. Ms. McDermott and Ms. Cotter[98] had been unemployed since 1983. They received unemployment benefit from January 1984 until January 1985. Then the payment was stopped on the grounds that a married woman was entitled to receive unemployment benefit only for a period of 312 days and at a lower rate than a married man. This law was neither amended nor declared null and void by 23 December 1983, the deadline for transposal. The High Court of the Republic of Ireland asked whether the claimants were – in the absence of transposition measures – entitled to receive the same benefits as those paid to married men directly on the basis of Article 4 of the directive. This was confirmed by the Court: "Article 4(1) ... could be relied on as from 23 December 1984 in order to preclude the application of any national provision inconsistent with it."

---

[97] *Dik, Menkutos-Demirci and Laar-Vreeman v. College van Burgemeester en Wethouders Arnheim and Winterswijk,* ECR 1988, p. 1601.

[98] Case 286/85, *McDermott and Cotter v. Minister for Social Welfare and Attorney-General (McDermott and Cotter I),* ECR 1987, p. 1453; see also Case C-377/89, *McDermott and Cotter v. Minister for Social Welfare and Another (McDermott and Cotter II),* ECR 1991, p. I-1155.

In the United Kingdom, a non-contributory invalidity pension was paid to married men who were incapable of work. Married women received the non-contributory invalidity pension only under the additional requirement that they were incapable of normal household duties. Ms. Clarke satisfied the condition of incapacity for work but did not satisfy the condition of incapacity for normal household duties. In its preliminary ruling, the Court recalled *McDermott and Cotter I* and declared that, in the absence of appropriate implementing measures, women must be granted precisely the same rights as men[99].

For cases of incapacity for work, the Netherlands Insurance Law stated that benefits were to be determined partly on the basis of marital status and the income earned from or in connection with the work of the spouse, or by the existence of a dependent child. Ms. Teuling[100] had worked for various employers from 1955 until 1972, when she became incapable of working. Until her husband died, she did not obtain family support supplements because account was taken of his income. Such a provision was regarded as consistent with Article 4(1) of Directive 79/7/EEC "if the system seeks to ensure adequate minimum subsistence income for beneficiaries who have a dependent spouse or children, by means of a supplement to the social security benefit which compensates for the greater burdens they bear in comparison with single persons".

3.4.4   Legitimate derogations from the principle of equality (Article 7)

Article 7(1) allows Member States to maintain different retirement ages for men and women with regard to old-age and retirement pensions and the possible consequences thereof for other benefits. Member States may also maintain certain sex-determined advantages, for instance for people who have brought up children, for the derived old-age or invalidity entitlements for wives, and for increased benefits for a dependent wife in cases of long-term invalidity, old age, accidents at work and occupational disease. The scope of this provision has been challenged in a number of preliminary rulings, which are outlined below.

In Belgium, the normal pensionable age used to be 65 years for men and 60 years for women. Entitlement to a retirement pension was acquired, for each year, at the rate of a fraction of salary with a denominator that

---

[99] Case 384/85, *Clarke v. Chief Adjudication Officer*, ECR 1987, p. 2865.
[100] Case 30/85, *Teuling v. Bedrijfsvereniging voor de Chemische Industrie*, ECR 1987, p. 2497.

could not be higher than 45 for men and 40 for women. A law of 1990 introduced a flexible retirement age and allowed all employees, both male and female, to take retirement at the age of 60. As regards the calculation of the amount of the pension, that law maintained the former rule. Mr. van Cant [101] claimed that the method of calculation placed him at a disadvantage in that he would not be entitled to a full pension until the age of 65, whereas a woman would reach that level by the age of 60. If he decided to retire at the age of 60, he would receive a lower pension than a woman of the same age.

The Court agreed with him that national legislation which prescribes a different method of calculating retirement pensions according to a worker's sex is discriminatory under Article 4(1) of Directive 79/7/EEC. Such discrimination can be justified on the basis of Article 7(1)(a) only if a difference in pensionable age between male and female workers has been maintained. If, on the contrary, national legislation has abolished the difference in pensionable ages for men and women, the Member State is not authorized to maintain a difference according to sex in the method of calculating the pension. Whether or not a Member State has abolished the difference in pensionable ages for men and women is a question of fact, which is for the national court to determine. In the case of Mr. van Cant, the claimant could rely directly on Article 4(1), because it was "unconditional and sufficiently precise" to grant direct rights. Mr. van Cant was entitled to the same method of calculation as women – with a denominator of 40 – as from 23 December 1984, the date on which the directive had to be transposed in the Member States.

The contributory state pension scheme in the United Kingdom used to require men to pay contributions for 44 years and women for 39 years in order to qualify for the same full basic retirement pension. Furthermore, a man working between the ages of 60 and 64 years paid contributions, whereas a woman in the same situation did not. The Equal Opportunities Commission [102] sought a declaration from the European Court of Justice that such a distinction on grounds of sex unlawfully discriminated against men. The Court interpreted the derogation referring to "the determination of pensionable age" as one that concerned the moment from which pensions became payable. The express purpose of

---

[101] Case C-154/92, *Van Cant v. Rijksdienst voor Pensioenen,* ECR 1993, p. I-3811; see also Joined Cases C-377/96 to C-384/96, *de Vriendt v. Rijksdienst voor Pensioenen,* ECR 1998, p. I-2105 and Case C-154/96, *Wolfs v. Office National des Pensions (ONP),* ECR 1998, p. I-6173.

[102] Case C-9/91, *The Queen v. Secretary of State for Social Security, ex-parte The Equal Opportunities Commission,* ECR 1992, p. I-4297.

Directive 79/7/EEC was to achieve progressive implementation of the principle of equal treatment for men and women in matters of social security. Its Article 7(1) intended to allow Member States to maintain temporarily the advantages accorded to women with respect to retirement in order to enable them to progressively adapt their pension system without disrupting its complex financial equilibrium. The Member State was authorized to determine the statutory pensionable age for old-age and retirement pensions according to sex. Forms of discrimination such as those described by the national court were necessarily linked to that difference and therefore in line with the directive.

The United Kingdom Social Security Act used to provide for the granting of severe disablement allowance to people who were incapable of work, and of invalid care allowance to people engaged in caring for a severely disabled person. Persons who had attained pensionable age – which was 65 years for men and 60 years for women – were generally excluded. Ms. Thomas [103] and four other women were refused severe disablement or invalid care allowance on the grounds that they had become invalid or applied for the benefits after having attained pensionable age.

The European Court of Justice reiterated that national legislation which denies women who have attained the age of 60 entitlement to benefits, whereas men continue to receive the benefit until the age of 65 years, is discriminatory and can be justified only by virtue of Article 7(1)(a) of Directive 79/7/EEC. As an exception from the principle of equality, the Court construed this provision strictly. Discrimination with respect to benefits other than old-age and retirement pensions could be justified only if it was "objectively necessary in order to avoid disrupting the complex financial equilibrium of the social security system or to ensure consistency between the retirement pension schemes and other benefit schemes". Thus:

> The scope of the permitted derogation, defined by the words 'possible consequences thereof for other benefits' contained in Article 7(1)(a), is limited to the forms of discrimination existing under the other benefit schemes which are necessarily and objectively linked to the difference in retirement age.

Again, the European Court of Justice left it to the national court to decide whether or not the difference in retirement age had been maintained, but gave guidance on the points to be considered. It stressed that the allowances in question were granted from a non-contributory system

---

[103] Case C-328/91, *Secretary of State for Social Security v. Thomas and Others*, ECR 1993, p. I-1247.

and had no direct impact on the financial equilibrium of the contributory pension schemes – criteria which indicated that the necessary linkage between the old-age pension and these allowances did not exist. In addition, the national rules prevented an overlap between the benefits in question and benefits paid to people who had insufficient resources, so the financial equilibrium of the social system was not endangered.

Italy used to set pensionable ages which differed according to sex. Pursuant to a law of 1981, a credit of contributions was granted for the period by which a worker fell short of the statutory early retirement scheme if an undertaking was declared to be in critical difficulty by the Interministerial Committee for Industrial Policy Coordination. This was the situation in the case of Ms. Balestra[104]. She challenged the scheme because she was entitled to the credit only until the age of 55 years, whereas male workers received the credit until the age of 60 years. This sex-related difference was accepted by the Court, "since the difference relating to sex in the method of calculating early-retirement benefits is objectively and necessarily linked to the setting of pensionable ages which differ for men and women".

Individual Member States are free to choose not to abolish the original discrimination but to alleviate it progressively by gradually improving the position of the disadvantaged sex. Such a rule was accepted as a legitimate derogation in the case of *Bramhill v. Chief Adjudication Officer*[105]. Once a Member State has abolished a distinction based on sex which had previously been allowed as an exception under Article 7(1), it cannot retain other associated forms of discrimination which existed only because of the former law.

The European Court of Justice looked at a number of concessions based on the condition of "pensionable age", this age being different for men and women. Mr. Taylor[106] was employed by the Post Office in the United Kingdom until he retired. He paid social security contributions throughout his working life. In 1998, aged 62 years and in retirement, he was in receipt of a Post Office pension. Under the national legislation, men of 65 years and over and women of 60 years and over who are already in receipt of certain state benefits, such as retirement or invalidity pension, are entitled to a winter fuel payment, a sum designed to help them pay

---

[104] Case C-139/95, *Balestra v. Istituto Nazionale della Previdenza Sociale (INPS)*, ECR 1997, p. I-549.

[105] Case C-420/92, ECR 1994, p. I-3191.

[106] Case C-382/98, *The Queen v. Secretary of State for Social Security, ex-parte Taylor*, see: http://curia.eu.int/en/actu/communiques/cp99/cp99100en.htm

their heating expenses during the winter. In its observations, the British Government argued that the national legislation sought only to provide protection against a lack of financial resources, and was therefore not affected by the rules of Community law relating to non-discrimination between men and women in matters of social security. This argument was not accepted. The payment was aimed at persons beyond the statutory age of retirement, which was 60 for women and 65 for men. It was designed to protect directly and effectively against the risk of old age, and consequently covered by Directive 79/7/EEC. But is a winter fuel payment "necessarily linked to the statutory age of retirement", as required by Article 7(1)? The Court denied such a link and considered the age distinction as contrary to Community law.

Another old-age pensioner in England, Mr. Richardson [107], retired at the age of 64 years, a year before the normal retirement age. He was required to pay prescription charges for the supply of drugs, medicines and appliances provided for by the United Kingdom National Health Service. Women between 60 and 65 years of age, unlike men in the same age bracket, were exempted from paying these charges. Mr. Richardson felt that he was discriminated against on the grounds of sex.

The European Court of Justice considered the exemption from payment of prescription charges as directly and effectively linked to the risks covered by Article 3(1). The difference based on sex with respect to a benefit other than statutory pensions could be justified only under the condition that it was "necessarily and objectively linked" to the difference in retirement age. There existed an inverse relationship between the exemption from prescription charges and the payment of National Insurance contributions inasmuch as persons who had reached pensionable age were no longer liable to pay these charges. The removal of the discrimination would not affect the financial equilibrium of the pension system. The Court therefore concluded:

> Article 7(1)(a) of Directive 79/7 does not allow a Member State which, pursuant to that provision, has set the pensionable age for women at 60 years and for men at 65 years also to provide that women are to be exempt from prescription charges at the age of 60 and men only at the age of 65.

Two recent rulings of the European Court of Justice concerned invalidity benefits paid to men and women under different age conditions.

---

[107] Case C-137/94, *The Queen v. Secretary of State for Health, ex-parte Richardson*, ECR 1995, p. I- 3407.

Ms. Hepple [108] received a reduced earnings allowance, a weekly benefit payable to persons who have suffered an occupational accident or disease. As from 1986, a retirement allowance replaced that benefit. The retirement allowance was paid only to persons who had not yet reached the retirement age of 65 years for men and 60 years for women. Women between 60 and 65 years of age received a lower allowance than men in comparable circumstances. This difference was accepted by the Court as a measure to ensure coherence between the retirement pension scheme and other benefits. The aim of the reduced earnings allowance and the retirement allowance was to compensate for a decrease in earnings. Male invalids aged 60 to 65 years did not receive a retirement pension, unlike women of the same age. This difference justified the assumption of a necessary link between the two schemes and the different age conditions for women and men.

In the case of *Buchner and Others v. Sozialversicherungsanstalt der Bauern* [109], the Court took another view. Austrian law provided that male farmers who were invalids were entitled to an early old-age pension from the age of 57 years, whereas female farmers who were invalids were entitled to the pension from the age of 55 years. Mr. Buchner claimed the benefit before he reached the age limit and was rejected. In this case, the Court denied a direct link between the minimum age for invalidity benefit and statutory retirement age. Women could claim the early old-age pension five years before the normal retirement age, while that period was eight years for men. Such an age distinction is contrary to Community law.

Thus, certain derogations from the principle of equality are permitted, but must be regularly reviewed. Member States may gradually reduce distinctions based on sex, but where national legislation has abolished the difference in pensionable age, the method of calculating the pension must be the same for both sexes. The derogation for pensionable ages may be extended to other benefits only if this is justified with respect to the financial equilibrium and interdependence of the schemes in question.

---

[108] Case C-196/98, *Hepple and Others v. Adjudication Officer*, ECR 2000, p. I-3701.

[109] Case C-104/98, ECR 2000, p. I-3625.

3.4.5 Justification of indirect discrimination in statutory social security schemes

Workers in irregular employment may be disadvantaged in statutory pension schemes, too. These schemes often prescribe minimum working hours, or minimum periods of membership, as preconditions for access to or benefits from the schemes. Such conditions are often not met by part-time, short-term, intermittent or job-sharing workers, the majority of whom are female. Can such *de facto* exclusion from state pensions be regarded as indirect discrimination based on sex?

Indirect discrimination is explicitly defined in Article 2(2) of Directive 97/80/EC. But the situations covered by Directive 79/7/EEC are excluded from the scope of Directive 97/80/EC (Article 3(1)). Nevertheless, although the definition of indirect discrimination does not apply *de lege lata*, it has been developed in case law and forms part of the *acquis communautaire*.

In matters of statutory social security, individual Member States have a broader margin of discretion than for matters of equal pay or equal treatment at the workplace. Article 4(1) of Directive 79/7/EEC precludes a national measure which, although formulated in neutral terms, works to the disadvantage of a much higher percentage of women than men or *vice versa*, unless it is based on objective factors unrelated to any discrimination on grounds of sex. The measures chosen must reflect a legitimate social policy aim of the Member State concerned, and be appropriate and necessary to achieve that aim. The Court obviously refrains from interfering too much in national policies that are highly sensitive, very costly, and based on particular social and historical conditions.

The case of Mr. Molenbroek [110] dealt with the award of a pension supplement paid under the Netherlands General Old-Age Law. The law provided that a married man or woman who was over 65 years of age and whose dependent spouse had not yet reached the age of 65 years would receive 70% of the net minimum wage. The insured pensioner was also entitled to a supplement up to a maximum of 30% of the net minimum wage, the supplement being reduced in accordance with the spouse's own income from or in connection with work. In the case of Mr. Molenbroek, the claimant's wife was receiving an incapacity

---

[110] Case C-226/91, *Molenbroek v. Bestuur van de Sociale Verzekeringsbank*, ECR 1992, p. I-5943.

allowance. That allowance was taken into consideration in calculating the supplement to his retirement pension, thus reducing his income. Mr. Molenbroek drew attention to the fact that the female partner was normally younger than the male, so the provision caused negative effects primarily to male old-age pensioners.

The Court noted that the rule in question was neither directly nor indirectly connected with the sex of the pensioner. The provision merely aimed at ensuring that the joint income of a married couple in which one spouse was of pensionable age at least equalled the income the couple would have when both had reached pensionable age. The Netherlands policy aimed at providing the persons concerned with a socially adequate income, regardless of possible additional income, and was justified. Similar rules of the Netherlands social assistance scheme were accepted in the cases of *Laperre*[111] and *Teuling*[112]. The latter case dealt with a system of benefits in respect of incapacity for work, under which the amount of the benefit was determined in part by marital status and the income earned in connection with the work of a spouse. The purpose of the system was to ensure an adequate minimum subsistence income for beneficiaries with a dependent spouse or children, by means of a supplement to the social security benefit which compensated for the greater burdens they bore in comparison with single persons.

In three important rulings, the Court accepted the thresholds fixed for access to the German statutory social security scheme. The first claimant, Ms. Nolte[113], had worked until 1965 and paid compulsory insurance contributions. She subsequently brought up her children and worked in "minor employment" as a cleaner. Owing to severe illness, Ms. Nolte was later prevented from working in "minor employment" and applied for a retirement and invalidity pension. Her claim was rejected because she was unable to show that she had paid 36 months' contributions in respect of employment subject to compulsory insurance. Ms. Megner and Ms. Scheffel[114] were both in minor and short-term employment and demanded to be insured in the compulsory statutory old age, sickness and unemployment insurance scheme. At the time in question, the German Social Insurance Code provided that "minor employment" was not subject to the statutory old age insurance scheme. Employment was

---

[111] Case C-8/94, *Laperre v. Bestuurcommissie Beroepszaken in de Provincie Zuid-Holland*, ECR 1996, p. I-273.
[112] See footnote 100.
[113] Case C-317/93, *Nolte v. Landesversicherungsanstalt Hannover*, ECR 1995, p. I-4625.
[114] Case C-444/93, *Megner and Scheffel v. Innungskrankenkasse Vorderpfalz*, ECR 1995, p. I-4741.

regarded as being minor where it was regularly engaged in for fewer than 15 hours per week and where a regular monthly income was below one-seventh of the average monthly salary of the persons insured (in 1993: DM 390 in the *new Länder* and DM 530 in the *old Länder*). These conditions were not met by the complainants.

Although Ms. Nolte had become incapable of working, she did belong to the working population in the meaning of Article 3(1) which refers to the risk of invalidity. Directive 79/7/EEC applies even if earnings are minimal and do not cover basic needs. In the working population as so defined, the majority of people in minor employment were female – so were the thresholds fixed by law indirectly discriminatory? The European Court of Justice denied this. It accepted the reasons put forward by the German Government, which related to structural principles and the compulsory nature of the scheme, and the social demand for "minor employment". Moreover, the Court stressed that social and employment policy was primarily a matter for the individual Member State.

3.5 Statutory pensions and equal treatment at the workplace

A difference in pensionable ages may lead to situations of unequal treatment at the workplace. The question is whether distinctions based on sex, permitted in state pension schemes by Directive 79/7/EEC, can be extended to situations governed by Directive 76/207/EEC in order to justify unequal treatment at the workplace. The first case that the Court dealt with on this question concerned an unequal age condition – linked with the normal pensionable age – for voluntary redundancy.

Mr. Burton was employed by British Railways[115]. His employer granted early pensions through an offer of voluntary redundancy under the following conditions: "Staff aged 60/55 (male/female) may leave the service under the redundancy and resettlement arrangements when the function in which [they are] employed has been dealt with under organisation planning." Mr. Burton applied for voluntary redundancy at the age of 58 years. His application was rejected on the grounds that he was

---

[115] Case 19/81, *Burton v. British Railways Board,* ECR 1982, p. 555; this ruling is problematic in view of the more recent case law on pensions in the public service and on Directive 76/207/EEC, see footnotes 120, 125 et seq.

under the minimum age of 60 years specified for male employees. He claimed that he was treated less favourably than female employees inasmuch as the benefit would have been granted to a woman of his age. Under United Kingdom legislation the minimum qualifying age for a state retirement pension was 60 years for women and 65 years for men. In the disputed clause, the right to voluntary early retirement was granted within the five years preceding the normal retirement age.

The European Court of Justice interpreted Article 5(1) of the Equal Treatment Directive, laying down the principle of equality with regard to working conditions, widely to include the conditions of termination of employment under a voluntary redundancy scheme. The option given to the employees was tied to the state scheme insofar as it made voluntary redundancy available during the five years preceding the minimum pensionable age fixed by national legislation. The fact that that age was not the same for men as for women was not regarded as unlawful, since the period was identical for women and men.

The case of Ms. Roberts posed the opposite problem. Is the employer entitled to grant early pensions under an equal age condition to men and women if the pensionable age is different? Ms. Roberts had been employed by Tate & Lyle [116] for 28 years and was dismissed at the age of 53 years under a mass redundancy. She and the other employees were members of an occupational pension scheme which was contracted out of the state pension scheme. It provided, for compulsory retirement, a pension at the age of 65 years for men and 60 years for women. All employees made redundant were offered either a cash payment or an early pension up to five years before their entitlement under the scheme, which was thus payable to men over the age of 60 years and to women over the age of 55 years. As a result of representations made by male employees alleging discrimination against men, Tate & Lyle agreed to grant an immediate pension to both men and women over the age of 55. Ms. Roberts brought the matter before an industrial tribunal, claiming that a male employee was entitled to the pension ten years before normal retirement age, whereas a female employee was entitled to the pension only five years before normal retirement age.

As in the *Burton* case, the Court considered the situation from the perspective of equal treatment at the workplace. The age condition was accepted, because it was precisely the same for women and men:

---

[116] Case 151/84, *Roberts v. Tate & Lyle Industries Ltd*, ECR 1986, p.703.

Article 5(1) of Directive 76/207/EEC must be interpreted as meaning that a contractual provision which lays down a single age for the dismissal of men and women under a mass redundancy involving the grant of an early retirement pension, whereas the normal retirement age is different for men and women, does not constitute discrimination on grounds of sex, contrary to Community law.

Ms. Marshall[117], a dietician employed by a British health authority, had expressed her willingness to continue to work beyond retirement age. At the age of 62 years, she was dismissed for the sole reason that she had reached the qualifying age for a statutory old- age pension. Ms. Marshall regarded this as discriminatory. The European Court of Justice was requested to say whether such a practice was in line with Community law, and whether Ms. Marshall was able to base her claim directly on Directive 76/207/EEC. The Court observed that the question on discrimination was not one of access to a statutory or occupational retirement scheme but one of equal treatment at the workplace. The dismissal of a woman solely because she has reached the qualifying age for a state pension, which is different for men and women, constitutes sex discrimination under the Equal Treatment Directive; it may be directly invoked against a state authority acting as an employer.

The same practice, but exercised by a privatized former public body, was at stake in *Foster and Others v. British Gas plc*[118]. The British Gas Corporation was operating as a statutory corporation and was privatized under the Gas Act 1986. Ms. Foster and her female colleagues were dismissed when they reached pensionable age, and the Court was requested to rule upon the direct applicability of Directive 76/207/EEC against a privatized body. The Court made reference to the *Marshall* case, stressing that an individual could rely on a directive against the State as employer regardless of the capacity in which the latter was acting. Whether as a private employer or in a public capacity, the State should not take advantage of its own failure to comply with the directive. The Court stressed that Article 5(1) was unconditional and sufficiently precise to be relied on against a body – whatever its legal form – which has been made responsible, pursuant to a measure adopted by the State, for providing a public service. These principles were later extended, in the *Beets-Proper* case, to private employers who do not deliver any service in the public interest.

---

[117] Case 152/84, *Marshall v. Southampton and South-West Hampshire Area Health Authority (Marshall I)*, ECR 1986, p. 723.

[118] Case C-188/89, ECR 1990, p. I-3313.

Ms. Beets-Proper was employed by F. van Lanschot Bankiers NV[119], a private bank. The employment relationship was governed by the collective agreement for the banking sector and the pension scheme of the bank's pension fund. The affiliated employees were entitled to an old-age pension from the date of retirement, which was 65 years for men and 60 years for women. Van Lanschot took the view that the employment relationship automatically ended by virtue of a condition implied in the collective agreement. Ms. Beets-Proper was no longer allowed to work when she reached pensionable age, and instituted proceedings. By virtue of the Equal Treatment Directive, the Court rejected the private employer's freedom to terminate employment on the grounds of reaching the qualifying age for retirement pension, if that age is different for women and men.

Ms. Kutz-Bauer[120] claimed the right to work beyond her pensionable age in a part-time scheme arranged under German law, which was based on a collective agreement with the City of Hamburg and financed partly by the Federal Institute of Labour. Public employees had the right to participate under the condition that they had not yet reached pensionable age. Ms. Kutz-Bauer's claim was rejected because she had applied to take part in the scheme beyond the age limit. Under the arrangement in question, both male and female workers could benefit from the scheme from the age of 55 years with the employer's consent. The great majority of the workers entitled to part-time employment for a period of five years from the age of 60 were male. The German Government argued that the aims of the scheme were to allow a smooth transition from work to retirement as well as to create opportunities for the recruitment of trainee workers and the unemployed. The additional financial burden associated with allowing female workers to take advantage of the scheme, even though they had already acquired entitlement to a retirement pension, would jeopardize the aims of the scheme.

This case was not a matter of statutory social security, where the Member States have a broad margin of discretion, but one of working conditions governed by Directive 76/207/EEC. Provisions of the kind in question result in discrimination against female workers unless they can be justified by objective factors unrelated to any discrimination based on sex. The Court observed that, although budgetary considerations may under-

---

[119] Case 262/84, *Beets-Proper v. F. van Lanschot Bankiers NV,* ECR 1986, p. 773.

[120] Case C-187/00, *Kutz-Bauer v. Freie und Hansestadt Hamburg,* judgement of 20 March 2003, see under: http://www.curia.eu.int/jurisp/cgi-bin/form.pl?lang=en

lie a State's choice of social policy and influence the nature or scope of social protection measures, they do not in themselves constitute an aim pursued by that policy and cannot therefore justify sex discrimination. Moreover, to concede that budgetary considerations may justify a difference in treatment would mean that the application and scope of the fundamental right of equal treatment between men and women might vary in time and place according to the state of the public finances of Member States. The Equal Treatment Directive therefore precludes:

> a provision of a collective agreement applicable to the public service which allows male and female employees to take advantage of a scheme of part-time work for older employees where under that provision the right to participate in the scheme of part-time work applies only until the date on which the person concerned first becomes eligible for a retirement pension at the full rate under the statutory old-age insurance scheme and where the class of persons eligible for such a pension at the age of 60 consists almost exclusively of women whereas the class of persons entitled to receive such a pension only from the age of 65 consists almost exclusively of men, unless that provision is justified by objective criteria unrelated to any discrimination on grounds of sex.

The Court took the opportunity to firmly stress the duties of the national judiciary in ensuring that the obligations arising out of the Treaty were fulfilled:

> In the case of a breach of Directive 76/207 by legislative provisions or by provisions of collective agreements introducing discrimination contrary to that directive, the national courts are required to set aside that discrimination, using all the means at their disposal, and in particular by applying those provisions for the benefit of the class placed at a disadvantage, and are not required to request or await the setting aside of the provisions by the legislature, by collective negotiation or otherwise.

The case *Meyers*[121] dealt with the relationship between the rights of equal access to work and to family benefit, and the consideration of childcare spending in the calculation of family benefit. Ms. Meyers, a single mother, claimed family credit in respect of herself and her daughter, then 3 years old. This benefit was awarded in order to supplement the income of low-paid workers who were responsible for a child. Her application was rejected on the ground that her income was greater than the level fixed for entitlement. Ms. Meyers submitted that childcare costs

---

[121] Case C-116/94, *Meyers v. Adjudication Officer*, ECR 1995, p. I-2131; see also Case C-63/91 and Case C-64/91, *Jackson and Cresswell v. Chief Adjudication Officer*, ECR 1992, p. I-4737.

were not deducted for the purposes of calculating her net income. She regarded this as indirect discrimination against single parents, and sex discrimination because most single parents who look after a child are women.

The question referred to the European Court of Justice was whether a benefit having the characteristics and purpose of such a family credit falls within the scope of Directive 76/207/EEC in terms of access to employment. The Court held that a scheme of benefits cannot be excluded from the scope of Directive 76/207/EEC solely because, formally, it is part of a social security system. Such a scheme may come within the scope of the directive if its subject matter is access to employment, vocational training, promotion, or working conditions. It was not sufficient that the conditions of entitlement were such as to affect the ability of a single parent to take up employment; the aim of the family credit went beyond that purpose. The aim was to ensure that families would not find themselves worse off in work than they would be if they were not working. The credit was intended to keep poorly paid workers in employment and therefore concerned access to employment, as referred to in Article 3 of the Equal Treatment Directive.

3.6   "Pay" or "statutory pension" in the public service?

Although pensions in the public service are often based on specific legislation, they are not regarded as the statutory pension schemes covered by Directive 79/7/EEC. The Court of Justice considers civil servants and public employees as a particular category of workers for whom the State, in its role as employer, should not be able to discharge its duties of respect for equal pay and equal treatment. Where contributions to and benefits from the public service pension funds are directly linked to the post previously occupied, they are generally regarded as "pay"[122].

The first ruling on contributions was on the case of *Liefting and Others*[123]. All claimants were Dutch civil servants whose spouses were also civil servants. The contributions to the old-age pension scheme were paid in

---

[122] For a household allowance under Luxembourg's Law on Remuneration of Civil Servants see Case 58/81, *Commission of the European Communities v. Grand Duchy of Luxembourg*, ECR 1982, p. 2175 (discrimination against female married civil servants who were entitled only when the husband was incapable of providing for the household expenses, while male civil servants received the allowance with no restriction).

[123] Case 23/83, *Liefting and Others v. Directie van het Academisch Ziekenhuis bij de Universiteit van Amsterdam*, ECR 1984, p. 3225.

the form of direct and indirect payments made by various public authorities, taking account of contributions made in respect of the spouse. Thus a female civil servant whose husband was also a civil servant had a lower gross salary. The Court ruled that it is contrary to the equal pay principle if consideration of the husband's income for a female civil servant leads to a lower gross salary of the woman, or if his higher gross salary directly affects the calculation of other benefits dependent on salary, such as severance pay, unemployment benefit, family allowances and loan facilities.

Dutch public servants' pensions were also under scrutiny in the *Beune*[124] case. The provisions applicable to the calculation of pensions had the effect that a married man's civil service pension was systematically lower than the civil service pension paid to a married woman of the same grade in the civil service. The Court did not accept this, because:

> Article 119 precludes legislation ... which ... lays down a rule for calculating the amount of the civil service pension for male married former civil servants which is different from that applicable to female married former civil servants; Article 119 may be relied on directly before the national courts; married men placed at a disadvantage by discrimination must be treated in the same way and have the same rules applied to them as married women.

Mr. Griesmar[125] challenged a provision of the French Civil and Military Pensions Code which provided that only a female civil servant received a service credit for the purpose of calculating retirement pension for each child she had brought up. Mr. Griesmar, the father of three children, received a retirement pension calculated merely on the basis of the years of service that he had actually completed. He took the view that he was the victim of unlawful sex discrimination, since the service credit, paid to female civil servants who are mothers in respect of each child, was not included in the calculation. The French government tried to justify this measure by claiming that the purpose of the credit was linked to the career-related disadvantages incurred during maternity leave. Mr. Griesmar argued that the credit was intended to offset disadvantages that resulted from bringing up a child, and that male civil servants who brought up children were likewise entitled to claim it.

---

[124] Case C-7/93, *Bestuur van het Algemeen Burgerlijk Pensioenfonds v. Beune*, ECR 1994, p. I-4471.

[125] C-366/99, *Griesmar v. French Republic*, ECR 2001, p. I-9383.

In an earlier equal pay case (*Abdoulaye and Others*[126]) the Court had indeed accepted that a lump sum payment could be granted by a private company to women on maternity leave, "where that payment is designed to offset the occupational disadvantages which arise for those workers as a result of their being away from work". But the requirement was different under the Civil and Military Pensions Code. The grant of this payment was in no way dependent on maternity leave; quite on the contrary, it was based on the longer period devoted to bringing up a child. In regard to the bringing-up of children, male and female civil servants are comparable; both face the same consequences for their careers. The Pensions Code did not establish a method for the calculation of retirement pension that was identical for both a female and a male civil servant, even when the latter was able to prove that he had brought up his children. This adversely affected the civil servants who were fathers and who had assumed the task of bringing up their children. A service credit granted at the date of their retirement cannot provide a remedy for the problems which women might encounter in the course of their professional career. Thus a distinction between the sexes in that respect could not be authorized as being a measure designed to help women in their career.

On the basis of the same Code, Mr. Mouflin [127], a French school teacher, claimed his retirement pension with immediate effect so as to be able to care for his wife who was suffering from an incurable illness. Under the challenged legislation, only a female – not a male – public servant was entitled to early retirement if her husband suffered from a disability or incurable illness which made it impossible for him to undertake any form of employment. The legislation did not accord that entitlement to a male public servant whose wife suffered from such a disability or illness. Mr. Mouflin was informed by the Minister for Education that "the right to retire to care for an invalid spouse is reserved exclusively to female civil servants".

In its judgement, the European Court of Justice confirmed that pensions provided under the French retirement scheme for civil servants fell within the scope of Article 119 EEC. This Article was infringed by a provision of national law prescribing that only female civil servants who take care of a spouse are entitled to a retirement pension with immediate effect. The situations of both sexes were comparable. According to

---

[126] Case C-218/98, *Abdoulaye and Others v. Régie nationale des usines Renault SA*, ECR 1999, I-5723.
[127] Case C-206/00, *Mouflin v. Recteur de l'Académie de Reims*, ECR 2001, p. I-10201.

the Court, there is no reason to distinguish the situation of a male civil servant whose wife suffers from a disability or incurable illness, making it impossible for her to undertake any form of employment, from that of a female civil servant whose husband suffers from such a disability or disease. The Court ruled that the provision in question discriminated against male civil servants on grounds of sex and constituted illegal discrimination in respect of pay.

Ms. Niemi[128] challenged a transitional provision which set a higher pensionable age for women than for men. The rule was based on the Finnish State Pension Act 280/1966 and applied to public servants enlisted in the defence forces. Previously, under the pension scheme that applied to public servants enlisted in the defence forces, the retirement age had been set at 60 years for women and 50 years for men. The scheme was amended by legislation which was enacted in 1994. Under the new scheme, posts of enlisted public servants are classified, according to the nature of their functions and without taking account of sex, as professional military posts and civilian posts. At retirement age, which is 55 for the first category and 65 for the second, an official must leave his or her post and is then entitled to an old age pension. A transitional provision for employment relationships dating from before 1 January 1995 set a retirement age between 50 and 55 years for men, depending on length of service, and 60 years for women. This transitional provision was applicable to Ms. Niemi.

The Finnish Government argued that one of the concerns was to guarantee to persons to whom the transitional rules applied the opportunity to obtain a pension at the full rate. The lowering of the age limit for female workers usually had the effect of reducing the amount of the pensions. The Court was not convinced, and applied Article 119 EEC in the claimant's favour. In respect of equal pay, the Court developed three criteria for the purpose of characterizing employment and benefits provided under a retirement scheme for civil servants: (a) existence of a link between the employment relationship and the retirement benefit; (b) a person is entitled to the pension in question only if his or her relationship to the employer is that of a public servant or ordinary employee; and (c) the pension benefits in question are calculated on the basis of pay. In the case of Ms. Niemi, these criteria were fulfilled, and she was entitled to a pension under the same conditions as men.

---

[128] Case C-351/00, *Niemi v. Valtion eläkelautakunta*, ECR 2002, p. I-7007.

The Court has given a ruling on an interesting case of sex discrimination. KB[129], a nurse, worked for the British National Health Service (NHS) for 20 years, during which time she paid contributions to the NHS pension scheme. The scheme provides for a survivor's pension to be payable to a member's surviving spouse. "Spouse" is defined as the person to whom the scheme member has been married. KB has shared an emotional and domestic relationship for a number of years with R, a person born a woman and registered as such in the Register of Births. Following surgical gender reassignment, R had become a man but had not been able to have his birth certificate amended to reflect that change officially. As a result, KB and R have not been able to marry. Their union was celebrated in an adapted church ceremony where they exchanged vows of the kind that would be made by any couple entering marriage. KB challenged the national legislation preventing transsexuals from marrying on the basis of their acquired gender in the context of the pay claim that she brought before the Employment Tribunal and the Court of Appeal. The latter court sought a preliminary ruling on the question of whether or not the exclusion of the transsexual partner of a female member of the NHS Pension Scheme, which limits the material dependant's benefit to her widower, constitutes sex discrimination in contravention of the principle of equal pay.

The Court delivered its judgement on 7 January 2004. It recalled that survivors' benefits granted under a pension scheme which essentially relates to the employment of the person concerned form part of the pay received by that person. The decision to restrict certain benefits to married couples while excluding all persons who live together without being married was a matter of national legislation and interpretation of domestic legal rules. Such a requirement could not be regarded *per se* as discriminatory on grounds of sex. However, the inequality of treatment did not relate to the award of a widower's pension but to a necessary precondition for the grant of such a pension: namely, the capacity to marry. The Court made reference to the case law of the European Court of Human Rights which regards such a denial as a breach of the right to

---

[129] Case C-117/01, *K.B. v. National Health Service Pensions Agency and Secretary of State for Health*, see ECJ Press Releases No 49/03 and No 04/04 under: http://www.curia.eu.int/ en/actu/communiques/index.htm. Full text published under: http://www.curia.eu.int/jurisp/cgi-bin/form.pl?lang=en&Submit=Suchen& docrequire= alldocs&numaff=C-117% 2F01&datefs=&datefe=&nomusuel=&domaine=&mots=&resmax=100. For dismissal of a transsexual worker see Case C-13/94, *P. v. S. and Cornwall County Council*, ECR 1996, p. I-2143. As regards the powers of the Community legislature in the context of same sex relationships see Case C-249/96, *Grant v. South-West Trains Ltd*, ECR 1998, p. I-621 (refusal of travel concessions to cohabitees of the same sex), and Case T-264/97, *D. v. Council*, CMLR 39, 2002, p. 51 (household allowance for a Community official living with a same sex partner).

marry under Article 12 of the *European Convention for the Protection of Human Rights and Fundamental Freedoms of 4 November 1950.* It concluded that the principle of equal pay precludes legislation which, in breach of that Convention, prevented a couple from fulfilling the marriage requirement which must be met for one of them to be able to benefit from part of the pay of the other.

3.7 Effective protection against sex discrimination — The payment of interest

Protection against discrimination must be rendered effective through suitable measures of redress or remedies, and criminal or civil sanctions. People whose right to equal pay has been violated must be treated like the comparative group. A number of cases have dealt with the consequences of breaches of the right to equal treatment at the workplace. The European Court of Justice decided that it is a matter of national law to determine the consequences for violations of the right to equal treatment, but the measures chosen must in any case be sufficient and adequate to make good the harm suffered by the victim, and have a deterrent effect[130]. Another problem particular to pension schemes is whether effective protection against discrimination – the *effet utile* – requires payment of interest.

This question came up in the case of Ms. Marshall, who was dismissed by her employer for the sole reason that she had reached pensionable age. It should be recalled that in the *Marshall I* case[131] the Court regarded the facts as direct discrimination, because male employees of the same age could continue working. Ms. Marshall's compensation claim was again referred to the Court, since it included, besides the loss of income, an additional sum of GBP 8,710 for interest and injury of feelings. The industrial tribunal dealing with the matter considered that it had no power to award the interest and immaterial damage. According to the Sex Discrimination Act 1975, compensation was limited to GBP 6,250, which the tribunal considered inadequate. The tribunal wished to accept Ms. Marshall's full claim of GBP 19,405 and brought before the European Court of Justice the question of whether the national legislation was in

---

[130] See footnote 70.
[131] See footnote 117.

line with Article 6 of Directive 76/207/EEC. This provision calls on the Member States to "introduce into their national legal systems such measures as are necessary to enable all persons who consider themselves wronged by failure to apply to them the principle of equal treatment... to pursue their claims by judicial process...". In its judgement on *Marshall II*[132], the Court shared the tribunal's view. It decided that:

> reparation of the loss and damage sustained by a person injured as a result of discriminatory dismissal may not be limited to an upper limit fixed *a priori* or by excluding an award of interest to compensate for the loss sustained by the recipient of the compensation as a result of the effluxion of time until the capital sum awarded is actually paid.

> A person who has been injured as a result of discriminatory dismissal may rely on the provisions of Article 6 of the Directive as against an authority of the State acting in its capacity as an employer in order to set aside a national provision which imposes limits on the amount of compensation recoverable by way of reparation.

The responsibility of a Member State for an infringement of Community law and the right to receive interest on arrears of social security benefits was brought before the Court in *The Queen v. Secretary of State for Social Security, ex-parte Eunice Sutton*[133]. Ms. Sutton was denied a non-contributory invalid care allowance, which she had claimed after reaching retirement age, that age being different for women and men. In *Thomas and Others*[134], the Court had declared that this practice constituted illegal sex discrimination by virtue of Directive 79/7/EEC. In addition to the arrears awarded to her, Ms. Sutton claimed interest. The authority dismissed that claim on the ground that national law did not provide for payment of interest on social security benefits. This problem was referred to the Court for preliminary ruling.

In this case, the Court employed a different approach from that in *Marshall II*. It drew attention to the fundamental difference between the reparation of damages lost and the principles of State liability. In cases of unequal treatment at the workplace, adequate compensation forms an essential component of redress. The same is not the case for arrears of social security benefits. Such benefits are paid by the competent bodies which must examine whether the conditions laid down in the relevant legislation are fulfilled by the person concerned.

---

[132] Case C-271/91, *Marshall v. Southampton and South-West Hampshire Area Health Authority (Marshall II)*, ECR 1993, p. I-4367.

[133] Case C-66/95, ECR 1997, p. I-2163.

[134] See footnote 103.

Consequently, the arrears paid do not constitute reparation for loss or damage sustained. The reparation is similar to other cases of State liability and must follow the same rules. By virtue of Community law, it must be paid where the provision infringed confers rights on the individual, where the breach is sufficiently serious, and when there is a causal link between the breach of the obligation resting on the State and the damage sustained by the injured party. Where those conditions are fulfilled, it is for the national court to decide upon the State's liability in accordance with national law. However, the reparation paid in cases of sex discrimination must not be less favourable than that provided for similar domestic claims, and must not be so framed as to make it virtually impossible or excessively difficult for the claimant to actually obtain it.

Conclusions

Sex equality is a fundamental European right. The European Court of Justice has developed innovative tools to translate this right into practical reality. It favours the concept of absolute equality. The principle of pay equality enshrined in the Treaty is interpreted broadly to cover occupational pension schemes, pensions in the public service and any other system designed for a particular category of workers.

For statutory schemes, Directive 79/7/EEC allows certain derogations from the principle of equality, but its scope is interpreted strictly. That instrument is generally not applied to pension schemes designed for a particular category of workers and pensions in the public service. In these fields of social security, members of the schemes may claim full equal treatment in terms of conditions, contributions and benefits. The Member States are required to periodically review and gradually remove distinctions based on sex. They must also grant access to justice and effective legal remedy. Even where distinctions between the sexes are permitted for statutory schemes, this does not justify different treatment of women and men at the workplace.

Unlawful discrimination in the field of social security persists and needs to be further addressed. Even today, decades after the adoption of the relevant directives, statistics on income, poverty and pensions show a clear disadvantage of women in terms of contributory social security benefits. In other areas such as survivors' benefits and retirement age, men are treated less favourably, being perceived as the family breadwinners. The European Court of Justice has created a legal framework for judicial interpretation, along with procedural mechanisms, to facilitate the pursuit of individual claims and the receipt of adequate compensation. However, these mechanisms are not sufficiently well known and applied, even among legal experts and the judiciary. More efforts are required to bridge the gap between equality on paper and everyday reality. In this process, the social partners, public bodies including the courts, and civil society all have an important role to play.

Annex A: Checklist for legal practitioners

Substantive issues

Main texts on sex equality in social security schemes

✔ Article 141 EC (ex Article 119 EEC) on equal pay

✔ Directive 75/117/EEC on equal pay

✔ Directive 76/207/EEC on equal treatment at the workplace

✔ Directive 2002/73/EC amending Directive 76/207/EEC (transposal deadline: 5.10.2005)

✔ Directive 79/7/EEC on equal treatment in statutory social security schemes

✔ Directive 86/378/EEC on equal treatment in occupational social security schemes

✔ Directive 96/97/EC amending Directive 86/378/EEC

✔ Directive 97/80/EC on the burden of proof in sex discrimination cases

The equal pay principle – Article 141 EC (ex Article 119 EEC) on equal pay and Directive 75/117/EEC

✔ "pay" means the "ordinary basic or minimum wage or salary and any other consideration, whether in cash or in kind, which the worker receives directly or indirectly, in respect of his [or her] employment, from his [or her] employer"

✔ grants an individual right

✔ can be directly invoked by an employee against any public or private employer *(Defrenne II)*

✔ interpreted broadly to include contributions to and benefits from occupational pension schemes, survivors' benefits, pensions in the public service and other schemes designed for a particular category of workers

✔ renders any direct distinction based on sex unlawful

✔ retroactive effect as from 8 April 1976 *(Defrenne II)* or more favourable national law *(Vick and Conze)*

✔ in cases of different age conditions for women and men with retroactive effect as from 17 May 1990 *(Barber)*

✔ renders any indirect discrimination unlawful *(e.g.* exclusion of part-time workers from occupational pensions) as from 8 April 1976 *(Defrenne II)* or more favourable national law or practice *(Vick and Conze)*

✔ effect: levelling up to the comparative group until replaced by a new – equal – scheme

Direct sex discrimination

✔ occurs where an explicit distinction is made between men and women, or where persons of male and female sex are treated differently in comparable situations

✔ discrimination based on "sex" covers unequal treatment of transsexual, but not of homosexual persons (discrimination based on "sexual orientation")

✔ a claimant can rely directly on Article 141 EC (ex Article 119 EEC), Article 1 of Directive 75/117/EEC, Article 2(1) of Directive 76/207/EEC and Article 4 of Directive 79/7/EEC

✔ direct pay discrimination cannot be justified

✔ direct discrimination at the workplace can be justified under Article 2(2)-(4) of Directive 76/207/EEC: where sex is a determining factor, for protection of women as regards pregnancy and maternity, or for promotional measures to remove existing inequalities

✔ direct discrimination can be justified under Directive 79/7/EEC for the protection of women on the grounds of maternity (Article 4(2)), or for lawful exclusions for determination of pensionable ages and certain advantages and benefits (Article 7)

✔ different calculation of statutory pensions is lawful only where a difference in pensionable age between men and women has been maintained; whether a State has abolished the age distinction is for the national court to decide

✔ direct discrimination can be justified under Directive 86/378/EEC for protection of women by reason of maternity and where Member States have deferred compulsory application (as amended by Directive 96/97/EC: only for self-employed workers)

✔ note: principle of equality is interpreted broadly, exceptions are interpreted restrictively

Indirect sex discrimination

✔ prohibited in all sex equality directives

✔ definition subsequent to *Bilka*: "where an apparently neutral provision, criterion or practice disadvantages a substantially higher proportion of the members of one sex unless that provision, criterion or practice is appropriate and necessary and can be justified by objective factors unrelated to sex"

✔ now: Article 2(2) of Directive 97/80/EC

✔ Directive 97/80/EC is not applicable for situations governed by Directive 79/7/EEC; the European Court of Justice accepts the negative effects of sex-neutral provisions in statutory pension schemes resulting from "necessary and appropriate means of achieving a legitimate objective of social policy" *(Megner, Scheffel, Nolte)*

Personal scope

✔ Article 141 EC (ex Article 119 EEC) and Article 1 of Directive 75/117/EEC: all workers or public and private employees in an employment relationship

✔ Article 1 of Directive 76/207/EEC: all employed men and women

✔ Article 2 of Directive 79/7/EEC: "the working population – including self-employed persons, workers and self-employed persons whose activity is interrupted by illness, accident or involuntary unemployment and persons seeking employment – and [to] retired or invalided workers and self-employed persons" (even if the risk covered by the directive has materialized in another person, *Drake*)

✔ Article 3 of Directive 86/378/EEC, as amended by Directive 96/97/EC: "members of the working population, including self-employed persons, persons whose activity is interrupted by illness, maternity, accident or involuntary unemployment and persons seeking employment, to retired and disabled workers and to those claiming under them, in accordance with national law and/or practice"

✔ "working population" includes workers whose earnings are not sufficient to cover their basic needs

✔ "working population" excludes persons who have never been in work, persons who have given up work to care for healthy spouses or children, and persons in non-paid domestic work

Material scope

✔ Article 141 EC (ex Article 119 EEC) and Article 1 of Directive 75/117/EEC: "pay", interpreted broadly to cover occupational pensions, pensions in the public service, survivors' pensions (*Podesta, Evrenopoulos, Griesmar, Mouflin, Niemi*)

✔ Article 1 of Directive 76/207/EEC: "equal treatment for men and women as regards access to employment, including promotion, and to vocational training and as regards working conditions and, on the conditions referred to in paragraph 2, social security"

✔ Article 3 of Directive 79/7/EEC: "(a) statutory schemes which provide protection against the following risks: sickness, invalidity, old age, accidents at work and occupational diseases, unemployment; (b) social assistance, in so far as it is intended to supplement or replace the schemes referred to in (a)"

✔ Article 2 of Directive 86/378/EEC, as amended by Directive 96/97/EC: "schemes not governed by Directive 79/7/EEC whose purpose is to provide workers, whether employees or self-employed, ... with benefits intended to supplement the benefits provided by statutory social security schemes or to replace them, whether membership of such schemes is compulsory or optional" (exclusion of individual contracts, optional benefits etc.)

✔ Statutory pensions and substituting or complementary social assistance benefits (Article 3(1) of Directive 79/7/EEC): Social assistance benefits must be directly and effectively linked to the protection provided against one of the risks specified in Article 3(1) of the directive

✔ Directive 79/7/EEC includes invalid care allowance paid because of another person's sickness or invalidity *(Drake)*

✔ Directive 79/7/EEC covers free medical prescription *(Richardson)* and winter fuel payment *(Taylor)*

✔ Directive 79/7/EEC does not cover: housing benefit *(Smithson)*, income support even where it replaces unemployment benefit, if availability for work is not required *(Jackson and Cresswell)*, concessionary fares on public transport *(Atkins)*

✔ Directive 79/7/EEC explicitly excludes: survivors' benefits, family benefits except for increases of benefits due in respect of the risks covered (Article 3(2)), and special favourable treatment on grounds of maternity (Article 4(2))

Possible derogations for determination of entitlement to pensions based on age and "the possible consequences thereof for other benefits" (Article 7 of Directive 79/7/EEC)

✔ extends to unequal contributions to national insurance schemes *(Equal Opportunities Commission)* as far as a difference in pensionable age has been maintained

✔ justifies distinctions based on sex that are objectively necessary in order to avoid disrupting the complex financial equilibrium of the social security system or to ensure consistency between retirement pension schemes and other benefit schemes

✔ does not justify restricting non-contributory benefits such as severe disablement and invalid care allowance to women under 60 years of age and men under 65 years of age *(Thomas and Others)*

✔ allows replacement of invalidity benefit with contributory retirement pension *(Graham)*

✔ reduced-earnings allowance can be linked to pension age if Member State puts forward convincing reasons for coherence between the systems *(Hepple, Buchner)*

✔ winter fuel payment *(Taylor)* and free medical prescriptions *(Richardson)* must be granted on equal age conditions to men and women

Legitimate derogations under Directive 79/7/EEC and equal treatment at the workplace under Directive 76/207/EEC

✔ dismissal because of reaching retirement age is prohibited under Directive 76/207/EEC *(Marshall, Beets-Proper, Foster)*

✔ access to a voluntary redundancy scheme *(Burton)*, to early old-age pension *(Roberts)* and to part-time work for older workers *(Kutz-Bauer)* must be granted on equal terms to men and women

✔ social benefits that aim at keeping workers in employment fall under Directive 76/207/EEC and must not indirectly discriminate against lone parents *(Meyers)*

Special focus: Governments

Pensions in the public service

✔ are "pay" if (a) a link exists between the employment relationship and the retirement benefit; (b) the entitlement to the pension derives from the relationship to the employer as public servant or ordinary employee; (c) and pensions are calculated on the basis of the pay

✔ no distinction based on sex is permitted with respect to retirement age, early retirement or invalidity pension, child-raising benefits or early retirement in order to care for invalid partner *(Griesmar, Mouflin, Niemi, Kutz-Bauer)*

Implementation of directives at the national level

✔ requires a total revision of related legislative and administrative rules at all State levels: national, regional, local

✔ where the aims of the directive are not sufficiently covered, existing rules must be amended or new legislation adopted

✔ all aims of a directive must be implemented comprehensively and effectively including provision for effective judicial remedy

✔ effective legal remedy must be provided to compensate for the material and immaterial harm suffered and to deter from discrimination

✔ access to independent justice must be enabled

✔ implementation deadline must be observed

✔ within additional time frame, texts of laws, regulations and administrative provisions adopted must be communicated to the Commission

✔ where derogations from the principle of equality are permitted, they should be restricted to the necessary extent, be explicit and periodically reviewed

✔ protection must be provided to prevent victimization

✔ in the fields of equal pay and equal treatment at the workplace (but not for social security and social protection) the social partners may be entrusted with the implementation of directives; the State retains ultimate responsibility

Member States are financially liable for incorrect transposal of a directive

✔ (a) when the result prescribed entails the grant of rights to individuals; (b) when the content of rights can be clearly identified by the provisions of the directive in question; and (c) when there is a causal link between the breach of State obligations and the damage sustained

✔ interest on arrears must be paid for violations of Directive 76/207/EEC (full reparation of damages, *Marshall II*)

✔ payment of interest on arrears for social security benefits under Directive 79/7/EEC must not be less favourable than provided for similar domestic claims *(Sutton)*

Special focus: Management and labour

Role of social partners

✔ in collective agreements: to ensure equal treatment in terms of working conditions, including dismissal, access to early retirement, part-time work for older workers, and redundancy schemes *(Marshall, Beets-Proper, Foster, Kutz-Bauer, Roberts, Burton)*

✔ to ensure equal pay in occupational pension schemes *(Barber* and *post-Barber)*

✔ to prevent indirect discrimination of part-time workers and other workers in non-standard forms of employment *(Bilka* and *post-Bilka)*

✔ social dialogue at Community level is promoted and facilitated by the Commission

✔ consulted on the possible direction of Community action in the social policy field and on the content of envisaged proposals

✔ to forward to the Commission, in the consultation process, an opinion or a recommendation

✔ can be entrusted, for working conditions and equal treatment between women and men at work (but not for pay as such, social security and social protection), with implementation of directives

✔ in the same areas, the social partners may conclude agreements at Community level

Special focus: The judiciary

Relevance of Community equality law in legal proceedings

✔ European equality legislation and case law must be considered *ex officio* by all courts or tribunals dealing with labour law, social law and the law governing the public service

✔ national provisions must be interpreted in the light of Community law, including the Treaty, the Charter of Fundamental Rights of the European Union, the aims of the relevant directives, and the rulings of the European Court of Justice

✔ limitations to rights must observe the principles of legality and proportionality

✔ even "soft law" which interprets European rights must be considered *(Grimaldi)*

✔ a national court must set aside any national provision that it considers contrary to Community law without having to wait until national legislation has been amended *(Defrenne II, Kutz-Bauer)*

✔ national courts which function as a last instance must refer a matter to the European Court of Justice where Community law might be relevant (Article 234 EC)

✔ the State is financially liable for manifest failure to apply that obligation *(Köbler)*

✔ reference to the European Court of Justice should be considered by all national courts, including the lower courts, in cases where Community law might be relevant and which have not yet been decided by the European Court of Justice

Directive 97/80/EC on the burden of proof in sex discrimination cases

✔ applies for situations covered by Article 141 EC (ex Article 119 EEC) and Directive 75/117/EEC, including occupational pensions and pensions in the public service, or any other scheme designed for a particular category of workers

✔ applies for situations covered by Directive 76/207/EEC on equal treatment at work

✔ applies, insofar as discrimination based on sex is concerned, for situations covered by Directive 92/85/EEC on maternity protection and Directive 96/34/EC on parental leave

✔ does not apply to the situations covered by Directive 79/7/EEC on statutory social security pensions (but applies for pensions covered by the equal pay principle)

✔ defines the concept of indirect discrimination: "where an apparently neutral provision, criterion or practice disadvantages a substantially higher proportion of the members of one sex unless that provision, criterion or practice is appropriate and necessary and can be justified by objective factors unrelated to sex" (Article 2(1))

✔ indirect discrimination in statutory pension schemes (Directive 79/7/EEC) is defined by case law as "any national measure which, although formulated in neutral terms, works to the disadvantage of a much higher percentage of women than men or vice versa, unless the measures chosen reflect a legitimate social policy aim, are appropriate to achieve that aim and are necessary in order to do so" *(Megner, Scheffel, Nolte)*

✔ it is a breach of Community law if national courts make it excessively difficult for claimants to pursue their rights granted under Community law *(Commission v. Italy)*

Annex B: The relevant legal instruments

CONSOLIDATED VERSION
OF THE TREATY
ESTABLISHING THE EUROPEAN COMMUNITY

Article 134

In order to ensure that the execution of measures of commercial policy taken in accordance with this Treaty by any Member State is not obstructed by deflection of trade, or where differences between such measures lead to economic difficulties in one or more Member States, the Commission shall recommend the methods for the requisite cooperation between Member States. Failing this, the Commission may authorise Member States to take the necessary protective measures, the conditions and details of which it shall determine.

In case of urgency, Member States shall request authorisation to take the necessary measures themselves from the Commission, which shall take a decision as soon as possible; the Member States concerned shall then notify the measures to the other Member States. The Commission may decide at any time that the Member States concerned shall amend or abolish the measures in question.

In the selection of such measures, priority shall be given to those which cause the least disturbance of the functioning of the common market.

TITLE X

CUSTOMS COOPERATION

Article 135

Within the scope of application of this Treaty, the Council, acting in accordance with the procedure referred to in Article 251, shall take measures in order to strengthen customs cooperation between Member States and between the latter and the Commission. These measures shall not concern the application of national criminal law or the national administration of justice.

TITLE XI

SOCIAL POLICY, EDUCATION, VOCATIONAL TRAINING AND YOUTH

CHAPTER 1

SOCIAL PROVISIONS

Article 136

The Community and the Member States, having in mind fundamental social rights such as those set out in the European Social Charter signed at Turin on 18 October 1961 and in the 1989 Community Charter of the Fundamental Social Rights of Workers, shall have as their objectives the promotion of employment, improved living and working conditions, so as to make possible their harmonisation while the improvement is being maintained, proper social protection, dialogue between management and labour, the development of human resources with a view to lasting high employment and the combating of exclusion.

To this end the Community and the Member States shall implement measures which take account of the diverse forms of national practices, in particular in the field of contractual relations, and the need to maintain the competitiveness of the Community economy.

87

24.12.2002 ⬚ EN ⬚ Official Journal of the European Communities C 325/93

They believe that such a development will ensue not only from the functioning of the common market, which will favour the harmonisation of social systems, but also from the procedures provided for in this Treaty and from the approximation of provisions laid down by law, regulation or administrative action.

Article 137 (*)

1. With a view to achieving the objectives of Article 136, the Community shall support and complement the activities of the Member States in the following fields:

(a) improvement in particular of the working environment to protect workers' health and safety;

(b) working conditions;

(c) social security and social protection of workers;

(d) protection of workers where their employment contract is terminated;

(e) the information and consultation of workers;

(f) representation and collective defence of the interests of workers and employers, including co-determination, subject to paragraph 5;

(g) conditions of employment for third-country nationals legally residing in Community territory;

(h) the integration of persons excluded from the labour market, without prejudice to Article 150;

(i) equality between men and women with regard to labour market opportunities and treatment at work;

(j) the combating of social exclusion;

(k) the modernisation of social protection systems without prejudice to point (c).

2. To this end, the Council:

(a) may adopt measures designed to encourage cooperation between Member States through initiatives aimed at improving knowledge, developing exchanges of information and best practices, promoting innovative approaches and evaluating experiences, excluding any harmonisation of the laws and regulations of the Member States;

(b) may adopt, in the fields referred to in paragraph 1(a) to (i), by means of directives, minimum requirements for gradual implementation, having regard to the conditions and technical rules obtaining in each of the Member States. Such directives shall avoid imposing administrative, financial and legal constraints in a way which would hold back the creation and development of small and medium-sized undertakings.

(*) Article amended by the Treaty of Nice.

The Council shall act in accordance with the procedure referred to in Article 251 after consulting the Economic and Social Committee and the Committee of the Regions, except in the fields referred to in paragraph 1(c), (d), (f) and (g) of this article, where the Council shall act unanimously on a proposal from the Commission, after consulting the European Parliament and the said Committees. The Council, acting unanimously on a proposal from the Commission, after consulting the European Parliament, may decide to render the procedure referred to in Article 251 applicable to paragraph 1(d), (f) and (g) of this article.

3.   A Member State may entrust management and labour, at their joint request, with the implementation of directives adopted pursuant to paragraph 2.

In this case, it shall ensure that, no later than the date on which a directive must be transposed in accordance with Article 249, management and labour have introduced the necessary measures by agreement, the Member State concerned being required to take any necessary measure enabling it at any time to be in a position to guarantee the results imposed by that directive.

4.   The provisions adopted pursuant to this article:

— shall not affect the right of Member States to define the fundamental principles of their social security systems and must not significantly affect the financial equilibrium thereof,

— shall not prevent any Member State from maintaining or introducing more stringent protective measures compatible with this Treaty.

5.   The provisions of this article shall not apply to pay, the right of association, the right to strike or the right to impose lock-outs.

Article 138

1.   The Commission shall have the task of promoting the consultation of management and labour at Community level and shall take any relevant measure to facilitate their dialogue by ensuring balanced support for the parties.

2.   To this end, before submitting proposals in the social policy field, the Commission shall consult management and labour on the possible direction of Community action.

3.   If, after such consultation, the Commission considers Community action advisable, it shall consult management and labour on the content of the envisaged proposal. Management and labour shall forward to the Commission an opinion or, where appropriate, a recommendation.

24.12.2002   EN   Official Journal of the European Communities   C 325/95

4.   On the occasion of such consultation, management and labour may inform the Commission of their wish to initiate the process provided for in Article 139. The duration of the procedure shall not exceed nine months, unless the management and labour concerned and the Commission decide jointly to extend it.

Article 139 (*)

1.   Should management and labour so desire, the dialogue between them at Community level may lead to contractual relations, including agreements.

2.   Agreements concluded at Community level shall be implemented either in accordance with the procedures and practices specific to management and labour and the Member States or, in matters covered by Article 137, at the joint request of the signatory parties, by a Council decision on a proposal from the Commission.

The Council shall act by qualified majority, except where the agreement in question contains one or more provisions relating to one of the areas for which unanimity is required pursuant to Article 137(2). In that case, it shall act unanimously.

Article 140

With a view to achieving the objectives of Article 136 and without prejudice to the other provisions of this Treaty, the Commission shall encourage cooperation between the Member States and facilitate the coordination of their action in all social policy fields under this chapter, particularly in matters relating to:

—   employment,

—   labour law and working conditions,

—   basic and advanced vocational training,

—   social security,

—   prevention of occupational accidents and diseases,

—   occupational hygiene,

—   the right of association and collective bargaining between employers and workers.

To this end, the Commission shall act in close contact with Member States by making studies, delivering opinions and arranging consultations both on problems arising at national level and on those of concern to international organisations.

Before delivering the opinions provided for in this article, the Commission shall consult the Economic and Social Committee.

(*) Article amended by the Treaty of Nice.

Article 141

1.   Each Member State shall ensure that the principle of equal pay for male and female workers for equal work or work of equal value is applied.

2.   For the purpose of this article, 'pay' means the ordinary basic or minimum wage or salary and any other consideration, whether in cash or in kind, which the worker receives directly or indirectly, in respect of his employment, from his employer.

Equal pay without discrimination based on sex means:

(a)   that pay for the same work at piece rates shall be calculated on the basis of the same unit of measurement;

(b)   that pay for work at time rates shall be the same for the same job.

3.   The Council, acting in accordance with the procedure referred to in Article 251, and after consulting the Economic and Social Committee, shall adopt measures to ensure the application of the principle of equal opportunities and equal treatment of men and women in matters of employment and occupation, including the principle of equal pay for equal work or work of equal value.

4.   With a view to ensuring full equality in practice between men and women in working life, the principle of equal treatment shall not prevent any Member State from maintaining or adopting measures providing for specific advantages in order to make it easier for the underrepresented sex to pursue a vocational activity or to prevent or compensate for disadvantages in professional careers.

Article 142

Member States shall endeavour to maintain the existing equivalence between paid holiday schemes.

Article 143

The Commission shall draw up a report each year on progress in achieving the objectives of Article 136, including the demographic situation in the Community. It shall forward the report to the European Parliament, the Council and the Economic and Social Committee.

The European Parliament may invite the Commission to draw up reports on particular problems concerning the social situation.

Article 144 (*)

The Council, after consulting the European Parliament, shall establish a Social Protection Committee with advisory status to promote cooperation on social protection policies between Member States and with the Commission. The tasks of the Committee shall be:

—   to monitor the social situation and the development of social protection policies in the Member States and the Community,

(*) Article amended by the Treaty of Nice.

24.12.2002   [EN]   Official Journal of the European Communities   C 325/97

— to promote exchanges of information, experience and good practice between Member States and with the Commission,

— without prejudice to Article 207, to prepare reports, formulate opinions or undertake other work within its fields of competence, at the request of either the Council or the Commission or on its own initiative.

In fulfilling its mandate, the Committee shall establish appropriate contacts with management and labour.

Each Member State and the Commission shall appoint two members of the Committee.

Article 145

The Commission shall include a separate chapter on social developments within the Community in its annual report to the European Parliament.

The European Parliament may invite the Commission to draw up reports on any particular problems concerning social conditions.

CHAPTER 2

THE EUROPEAN SOCIAL FUND

Article 146

In order to improve employment opportunities for workers in the internal market and to contribute thereby to raising the standard of living, a European Social Fund is hereby established in accordance with the provisions set out below; it shall aim to render the employment of workers easier and to increase their geographical and occupational mobility within the Community, and to facilitate their adaptation to industrial changes and to changes in production systems, in particular through vocational training and retraining.

Article 147

The Fund shall be administered by the Commission.

The Commission shall be assisted in this task by a Committee presided over by a Member of the Commission and composed of representatives of governments, trade unions and employers' organisations.

Article 148

The Council, acting in accordance with the procedure referred to in Article 251 and after consulting the Economic and Social Committee and the Committee of the Regions, shall adopt implementing decisions relating to the European Social Fund.

II

(Acts whose publication is not obligatory)

COUNCIL

COUNCIL DIRECTIVE

of 10 February 1975

on the approximation of the laws of the Member States relating to the application of the principle of equal pay for men and women

(75/117/EEC)

THE COUNCIL OF THE EUROPEAN COMMUNITIES,

Having regard to the Treaty establishing the European Economic Community, an in particular Article 100 thereof ;

Having regard to the proposal from the Commission ;

Having regard to the Opinion of the European Parliament (¹) ;

Having regard to the Opinion of the Economic and Social Committee (²) ;

Whereas implementation of the principle that men and women should receive equal pay contained in Article 119 of the Treaty is an integral part of the establishment and functioning of the common market ;

Whereas it is primarily the responsibility of the Member States to ensure the application of this principle by means of appropriate laws, regulations and administrative provisions ;

Whereas the Council resolution of 21 January 1974 (³) concerning a social action programme, aimed at making it possible to harmonize living and working conditions while the improvement is being maintained and at achieving a balanced social and economic development of the Community, recognized that priority should be given to action taken on behalf of women as regards access to employment and vocational training and advancement, and as regards working conditions, including pay ;

Whereas it is desirable to reinforce the basic laws by standards aimed at facilitating the pratical application of the principle of equality in such a way that all employees in the Community can be protected in these matters ;

Whereas differences continue to exist in the various Member States despite the efforts made to apply the resolution of the conference of the Member States of 30 December 1961 on equal pay for men and women and whereas, therefore, the national provisions should be approximated as regards application of the principle of equal pay,

HAS ADOPTED THIS DIRECTIVE :

Article 1

The principle of equal pay for men and women outlined in Article 119 of the Treaty, hereinafter called 'principle of equal pay', means, for the same work or for work to which equal value is attributed, the elimination of all discrimination on grounds of sex with regard to all aspects and conditions of remuneration.

In particular, where a job classification system is used for determining pay, it must be based on the same criteria for both men and women and so drawn up as to exclude any discrimination on grounds of sex.

(¹) OJ No C 55, 13. 5. 1974, p. 43.
(²) OJ No C 88, 26. 7. 1974, p. 7.
(³) OJ No C 13, 12. 2. 1974, p. 1.

Gender roles and sex equality: European solutions to social security disputes

Article 2

Member States shall introduce into their national legal systems such measures as are necessary to enable all employees who consider themselves wronged by failure to apply the principle of equal pay to pursue their claims by judicial process after possible recourse to other competent authorities.

Article 3

Member States shall abolish all discrimination between men and women arising from laws, regulations or administrative provisions which is contrary to the principle of equal pay.

Article 4

Member States shall take the necessary measures to ensure that provisions appearing in collective agreements, wage scales, wage agreements or individual contracts of employment which are contrary to the principle of equal pay shall be, or may be declared, null and void or may be amended.

Article 5

Member States shall take the necessary measures to protect employees against dismissal by the employer as a reaction to a complaint within the undertaking or to any legal proceedings aimed at enforcing compliance with the principle of equal pay.

Article 6

Member States shall, in accordance with their national circumstances and legal systems, take the measures necessary to ensure that the principle of equal pay is applied. They shall see that effective means are available to take care that this principle is observed.

Article 7

Member States shall take care that the provisions adopted pursuant to this Directive, together with the relevant provisions already in force, are brought to the attention of employees by all appropriate means, for example at their place of employment.

Article 8

1. Member States shall put into force the laws, regulations and administrative provisions necessary in order to comply with this Directive within one year of its notification and shall immediately inform the Commission thereof.

2. Member States shall communicate to the Commission the texts of the laws, regulations and administrative provisions which they adopt in the field covered by this Directive.

Article 9

Within two years of the expiry of the one-year period referred to in Article 8, Member States shall forward all necessary information to the Commission to enable it to draw up a report on the application of this Directive for submission to the Council.

Article 10

This Directive is addressed to the Member States.

Done at Brussels, 10 February 1975.

For the Council

The President

G. FITZGERALD

COUNCIL DIRECTIVE

of 9 February 1976

on the implementation of the principle of equal treatment for men and women as regards access to employment, vocational training and promotion, and working conditions

(76/207/EEC)

THE COUNCIL OF THE EUROPEAN COMMUNITIES,

Having regard to the Treaty establishing the European Economic Community, and in particular Article 235 thereof,

Having regard to the proposal from the Commission,

Having regard to the opinion of the European Parliament [1],

Having regard to the opinion of the Economic and Social Committee [2],

Whereas the Council, in its resolution of 21 January 1974 concerning a social action programme [3], included among the priorities action for the purpose of achieving equality between men and women as regards access to employment and vocational training and promotion and as regards working conditions, including pay;

Whereas, with regard to pay, the Council adopted on 10 February 1975 Directive 75/117/EEC on the approximation of the laws of the Member States relating to the application of the principle of equal pay for men and women [4];

Whereas Community action to achieve the principle of equal treatment for men and women in respect of access to employment and vocational training and promotion and in respect of other working conditions also appears to be necessary; whereas, equal treatment for male and female workers constitutes one of the objectives of the Community, in so far as the harmonization of living and working conditions while maintaining their improvement are *inter alia* to be furthered; whereas the Treaty does not confer the necessary specific powers for this purpose;

Whereas the definition and progressive implementation of the principle of equal treatment in matters of social security should be ensured by means of subsequent instruments,

[1] OJ No C 111, 20. 5. 1975, p. 14.
[2] OJ No C 286, 15. 12. 1975, p. 8.
[3] OJ No C 13, 12. 2. 1974, p. 1.
[4] OJ No L 45, 19. 2. 1975, p. 19.

HAS ADOPTED THIS DIRECTIVE:

Article 1

1. The purpose of this Directive is to put into effect in the Member States the principle of equal treatment for men and women as regards access to employment, including promotion, and to vocational training and as regards working conditions and, on the conditions referred to in paragraph 2, social security. This principle is herinafter referred to as 'the principle of equal treatment.'

2. With a view to ensuring the progressive implementation of the principle of equal treatment in matters of social security, the Council, acting on a proposal from the Commission, will adopt provisions defining its substance, its scope and the arrangements for its application.

Article 2

1. For the purposes of the following provisions, the principle of equal treatment shall mean that there shall be no discrimination whatsover on grounds of sex either directly or indirectly by reference in particular to marital or family status.

2. This Directive shall be without prejudice to the right of Member States to exclude from its field of application those occupational activities and, where appropriate, the training leading thereto, for which, by reason of their nature or the context in which they are carried out, the sex of the worker constitutes a determining factor.

3. This Directive shall be without prejudice to provisions concerning the protection of women, particularly as regards pregnancy and maternity.

4. This Directive shall be without prejudice to measures to promote equal opportunity for men and women, in particular by removing existing inequalities which affect women's opportunities in the areas referred to in Article 1 (1).

14. 2. 76   Official Journal of the European Communities   No L 39/41

Article 3

1. Application of the principle of equal treatment means that there shall be no discrimination whatsover on grounds of sex in the conditions, including selection criteria, for access to all jobs or posts, whatever the sector or branch of activity, and to all levels of the occupational hierarchy.

2. To this end, Member States shall take the measures necessary to ensure that :

(a) any laws, regulations and administrative provisions contrary to the principle of equal treatment shall be abolished ;

(b) any provisions contrary to the principle of equal treatment which are included in collective agreements, individual contracts of employment, internal rules of undertakings or in rules governing the independent occupations and professions shall be, or may be declared, null and void or may be amended ;

(c) those laws, regulations and administrative provisions contrary to the principle of equal treatment when the concern for protection which originally inspired them is no longer well founded shall be revised ; and that where similar provisions are included in collective agreements labour and management shall be requested to undertake the desired revision.

Article 4

Application of the principle of equal treatment with regard to access to all types and to all levels, of vocational guidance, vocational training, advanced vocational training and retraining, means that Member States shall take all necessary measures to ensure that :

(a) any laws, regulations and administrative provisions contrary to the principle of equal treatment shall be abolished ;

(b) any provisions contrary to the principle of equal treatment which are included in collective agreements, individual contracts of employment, internal rules of undertakings or in rules governing the independent occupations and professions shall be, or may be declared, null and void or may be amended ;

(c) without prejudice to the freedom granted in certain Member States to certain private training establishments, vocational guidance, · vocational training, advanced vocational training and retraining shall be accessible on the basis of the same criteria and at the same levels without any discrimination on grounds of sex.

Article 5

1. Application of the principle of equal treatment with regard to working conditions, including the conditions governing dismissal, means that men and women shall be guaranteed the same conditions without discrimination on grounds of sex.

2. To this end, Member States shall take the measures necessary to ensure that :

(a) any laws, regulations and administrative provisions contrary to the principle of equal treatment shall be abolished ;

(b) any provisions contrary to the principle of equal treatment which are included in collective agreements, individual contracts of employment, internal rules of undertakings or in rules governing the independent occupations and professions shall be, or may be declared, null and void or may be amended ;

(c) those laws, regulations and ·administrative provisions contrary to the principle of equal treatment when the concern for protection which originally inspired them is no longer well founded shall be revised ; and that where similar provisions are included in collective agreements labour and management shall be requested to undertake the desired revision.

Article 6

Member States shall introduce into their national legal systems such measures as are necessary to enable all persons who consider themselves wronged by failure to apply to them the principle of equal treatment within the meaning of Articles 3, 4 and 5 to pursue their claims by judicial process after possible recourse to other competent authorities.

Article 7

Member States shall take the necessary measures to protect employees against dismissal by the employer as a reaction to-a complaint within the undertaking or to any legal proceedings aimed at enforcing compliance with the principle of equal treatment.

Article 8

Member States shall take care that the provisions adopted pursuant to this Directive, together with the relevant provisions already in force, are brought to the attention of employees by all appropriate means, for example at their place of employment.

Article 9

1. Member States shall put into force the laws, regulations and administrative provisions necessary in order to comply with this Directive within 30 months of its notification and shall immediately inform the Commission thereof.

However, as regards the first part of Article 3 (2) (c) and the first part of Article 5 (2) (c), Member States shall carry out a first examination and if necessary a first revision of the laws, regulations and administrative provisions referred to therein within four years of notification of this Directive.

2.   Member States shall periodically assess the occupational activities referred to in Article 2 (2) in order to decide, in the light of social developments, whether there is justification for maintaining the exclusions concerned. They shall notify the Commission of the results of this assessment.

3.   Member States shall also communicate to the Commission the texts of laws, regulations and administrative provisions which they adopt in the field covered by this Directive.

Article 10

Within two years following expiry of the 30-month period laid down in the first subparagraph of Article 9 (1), Member States shall forward all necessary information to the Commission to enable it to draw up a report on the application of this Directive for submission to the Council.

Article 11

This Directive is addressed to the Member States.

Done at Brussels, 9 February 1976.

For the Council

The President

G. THORN

No L 6/24   Official Journal of the European Communities   10. 1. 79

COUNCIL DIRECTIVE

of 19 December 1978

on the progressive implementation of the principle of equal treatment for men and women in matters of social security

(79/7/EEC)

THE COUNCIL OF THE EUROPEAN COMMUNITIES,

Having regard to the Treaty establishing the European Economic Community, and in particular Article 235 thereof,

Having regard to the proposal from the Commission (¹),

Having regard to the opinion of the European Parliament (²),

Having regard to the opinion of the Economic and Social Committee (³),

Whereas Article 1 (2) of Council Directive 76/207/EEC of 9 February 1976 on the implementation of the principle of equal treatment for men and women as regards access to employment, vocational training and promotion, and working conditions (⁴) provides that, with a view to ensuring the progressive implementation of the principle of equal treatment in matters of social security, the Council, acting on a proposal from the Commission, will adopt provisions defining its substance, its scope and the arrangements for its application ; whereas the Treaty does not confer the specific powers required for this purpose ;

Whereas the principle of equal treatment in matters of social security should be implemented in the first place in the statutory schemes which provide protection against the risks of sickness, invalidity, old age, accidents at work, occupational diseases and unemployment, and in social assistance in so far as it is intended to supplement or replace the abovementioned schemes ;

Whereas the implementation of the principle of equal treatment in matters of social security does not prejudice the provisions relating to the protection of women on the ground of maternity ; whereas, in this respect, Member States may adopt specific provisions for women to remove existing instances of unequal treatment,

(¹) OJ No C 34, 11. 2. 1977, p. 3.
(²) OJ No C 299, 12. 12. 1977, p. 13.
(³) OJ No C 180, 28. 7. 1977, p. 36.
(⁴) OJ No L 39, 14. 2. 1976, p. 40.

HAS ADOPTED THIS DIRECTIVE :

Article 1

The purpose of this Directive is the progressive implementation, in the field of social security and other, elements of social protection provided for in Article 3, of the principle of equal treatment for men and women in matters of social security, hereinafter referred to as 'the principle of equal treatment'.

Article 2

This Directive shall apply to the working population — including self-employed persons, workers and self-employed persons whose activity is interrupted by illness, accident or involuntary unemployment and persons seeking employment — and to retired or invalided workers and self-employed persons.

Article 3

1. This Directive shall apply to :

(a) statutory schemes which provide protection against the following risks :

— sickness,
— invalidity,
— old age,
— accidents at work and occupational diseases,
— unemployment ;

(b) social assistance, in so far as it is intended to supplement or replace the schemes referred to in (a).

2. This Directive shall not apply to the provisions concerning survivors' benefits nor to those concerning family benefits, except in the case of family benefits granted by way of increases of benefits due in respect of the risks referred to in paragraph 1 (a).

3. With a view to ensuring implementation of the principle of equal treatment in occupational schemes, the Council, acting on a proposal from the Commission, will adopt provisions defining its substance, its scope and the arrangements for its application.

Article 4

1. The principle of equal treatment means that there shall be no discrimination whatsoever on ground of sex either directly, or indirectly by reference in particular to marital or family status, in particular as concerns :

— the scope of the schemes and the conditions of access thereto,

— the obligation to contribute and the calculation of contributions,

— the calculation of benefits including increases due in respect of a spouse and for dependants and the conditions governing the duration and retention of entitlement to benefits.

2. The principle of equal treatment shall be without prejudice to the provisions relating to the protection of women on the grounds of maternity.

Article 5

Member States shall take the measures necessary to ensure that any laws, regulations and administrative provisions contrary to the principle of equal treatment are abolished.

Article 6

Member States shall introduce into their national legal systems such measures as are necessary to enable all persons who consider themselves wronged by failure to apply the principle of equal treatment to pursue their claims by judicial process, possibly after recourse to other competent authorities.

Article 7

1. This Directive shall be without prejudice to the right of Member States to exclude from its scope :

(a) the determination of pensionable age for the purposes of granting old-age and retirement pensions and the possible consequences thereof for other benefits ;

(b) advantages in respect of old-age pension schemes granted to persons who have brought up children ; the acquisition of benefit entitlements following periods of interruption of employment due to the bringing up of children ;

(c) the granting of old-age or invalidity benefit entitlements by virtue of the derived entitlements of a wife ;

(d) the granting of increases of long-term invalidity, old-age, accidents at work and occupational disease benefits for a dependent wife ;

(e) the consequences of the exercise, before the adoption of this Directive, of a right of option not to acquire rights or incur obligations under a statutory scheme.

2. Member States shall periodically examine matters excluded under paragraph 1 in order to ascertain, in the light of social developments in the matter concerned, whether there is justification for maintaining the exclusions concerned.

Article 8

1. Member States shall bring into force the laws, regulations and administrative provisions necessary to comply with this Directive within six years of its notification. They shall immediately inform the Commission thereof.

2. Member States shall communicate to the Commission the text of laws, regulations and administrative provisions which they adopt in the field covered by this Directive, including measures adopted pursuant to Article 7 (2).

They shall inform the Commission of their reasons for maintaining any existing provisions on the matters referred to in Article 7 (1) and of the possibilities for reviewing them at a later date.

Article 9

Within seven years of notification of this Directive, Member States shall forward all information necessary to the Commission to enable it to draw up a report on the application of this Directive for submission to the Council and to propose such further measures as may be required for the implementation of the principle of equal treatment.

Article 10

This Directive is addressed to the Member States.

Done at Brussels, 19 December 1978.

For the Council

The President

H.-D. GENSCHER

No L 225/40   Official Journal of the European Communities   12. 8. 86

II

(Acts whose publication is not obligatory)

COUNCIL

COUNCIL DIRECTIVE
of 24 July 1986
on the implementation of the principle of equal treatment for men and women in occupational social security schemes

(86/378/EEC)

THE COUNCIL OF THE EUROPEAN COMMUNITIES,

Having regard to the Treaty establishing the European Economic Community, and in particular Articles 100 and 235 thereof,

Having regard to the proposal from the Commission (¹),

Having regard to the opinion of the European Parliament (²),

Having regard to the opinion of the Economic and Social Committee (³),

Whereas the Treaty provides that each Member State shall ensure the application of the principle that men and women should receive equal pay for equal work ; whereas 'pay' should be taken to mean the ordinary basic or minimum wage or salary and any other consideration, whether in cash or in kind, which the worker receives, directly or indirectly, from his employer in respect of his employment ;

Whereas, although the principle of equal pay does indeed apply directly in cases where discrimination can be determined solely on the basis of the criteria of equal treatment and equal pay, there are also situations in which implementation of this principle implies the adoption of additional measures which more clearly define its scope ;

Whereas Article 1 (2) of Council Directive 76/207/EEC of 9 February 1976 on the implementation of the principle

of equal treatment for men and women as regards access to employment, vocational training and promotion, and working conditions (⁴) provides that, with a view to ensuring the progressive implementation of the principle of equal treatment in matters of social security, the Council, acting on a proposal from the Commission, will adopt provisions defining its substance, its scope and the arrangements for its application ; whereas the Council adopted to this end Directive 79/7/EEC of 19 December 1978 on the progressive implementation of the principle of equal treatment for men and women in matters of social security (⁵) ;

Whereas Article 3 (3) of Directive 79/7/EEC provides that, with a view to ensuring implementation of the principle of equal treatment in occupational schemes, the Council, acting on a proposal from the Commission, will adopt provisions defining its substance, its scope and the arrangements for its application ;

Whereas the principle of equal treatment should be implemented in occupational social security schemes which provide protection against the risks specified in Article 3 (1) of Directive 79/7/EEC as well as those which provide employees with any other consideration in cash or in kind within the meaning of the Treaty ;

Whereas implementation of the principle of equal treatment does not prejudice the provisions relating to the protection of women by reason of maternity,

(¹) OJ No C 134, 21. 5. 1983, p. 7.
(²) OJ No C 117, 30. 4. 1984, p. 169.
(³) OJ No C 35, 9. 2. 1984, p. 7.

(⁴) OJ No L 39, 14. 2. 1976, p. 40.
(⁵) OJ No L 6, 10. 1. 1979, p. 24.

HAS ADOPTED THIS DIRECTIVE:

Article 1

The object of this Directive is to implement, in occupational social security schemes, the principle of equal treatment for men and women, hereinafter referred to as 'the principle of equal treatment'.

Article 2

1. 'Occupational social security schemes' means schemes not governed by Directive 79/7/EEC whose purpose is to provide workers, whether employees or self-employed, in an undertaking or group of undertakings, area of economic activity or occupational sector or group of such sectors with benefits intended to supplement the benefits provided by statutory social security schemes or to replace them, whether membership of such schemes is compulsory or optional.

2. This Directive does not apply to:

(a) individual contracts,

(b) schemes having only one member,

(c) in the case of salaried workers, insurance schemes offered to participants individually to guarantee them:

— either additional benefits, or

— a choice of date on which the normal benefits will start, or a choice between several benefits.

Article 3

This Directive shall apply to members of the working population including self-employed persons, persons whose activity is interrupted by illness, matrnity, accident or involuntary unemployment and persons seeking employment, and to retired and disabled workers.

Article 4

This Directive shall apply to:

(a) occupational schemes which provide protection against the following risks:

— sickness,

— invalidity,

— old age, including early retirement,

— industrial accidents and occupational diseases,

— unemployment;

(b) occupational schemes which provide for other social benefits, in cash or in kind, and in particular survivors' benefits and family allowances, if such benefits are accorded to employed persons and thus constitute a consideration paid by the employer to the worker by reason of the latter's employment.

Article 5

1. Unter the conditions laid down in the following provisions, the principle of equal treatment implies that there shall be no discrimination on the basis of sex, either directly or indirectly, by reference in particular to marital or family status, especially as regards:

— the scope of the schemes and the conditions of access to them;

— the obligation to contribute and the calculation of contributions;

— the calculation of benefits, including supplementary benefits due in respect of a spouse or dependants, and the conditions governing the duration and retention of entitlement to benefits.

2. The principle of equal treatment shall not prejudice the provisions relating to the protection of women by reason of maternity.

Article 6

1. Provisions contrary to the principle of equal treatment shall include those based on sex, either directly or indirectly, in particular by reference to marital or family for:

(a) determining the persons who may participate in an occupational scheme;

(b) fixing the compulsory or optional nature of participation in an occupational scheme;

(c) laying down different rules as regards the age of entry into the scheme or the minimum period of employment or membership of the scheme required to obtain the benefits thereof;

(d) laying down different rules, except as provided for in subparagraphs (h) and (i), for the reimbursement of contributions where a worker leaves a scheme without having fulfilled the conditions guaranteeing him a deferred right to long-term benefits;

(e) setting different conditions for the granting of benefits of restricting such benefits to workers of one or other of the sexes;

(f) fixing different retirement ages;

(g) suspending the retention or acquisition of rights during periods of maternity leave or leave for family reasons which are granted by law or agreement and are paid by the employer;

(h) setting different levels of benefit, except insofar as may be necessary to take account of actuarial calculation factors which differ according to sex in the case of benefits designated as contribution-defined;

No L 225/42   Official Journal of the European Communities   12. 8. 86

(i) setting different levels of worker contribution;

setting different levels of employer contribution in the case of benefits designated as contribution-defined, except with a view to making the amount of those benefits more nearly equal;

(j) laying down different standards or standards applicable only to workers of a specified sex, except as provided for in subparagraphs (h) and (i), as regards the guarantee or retention of entitlement to deferred benefits when a worker leaves a scheme.

2. Where the granting of benefits within the scope of this Directive is left to the discretion of the scheme's management bodies, the latter must take account of the principle of equal treatment.

Article 7

Member States shall take all necessary steps to ensure that:

(a) provisions contrary to the principle of equal treatment in legally compulsory collective agreements, staff rules of undertakings or any other arrangements relating to occupational schemes are null and void, or may be declared null and void or amended;

(b) schemes containing such provisions may not be approved or extended by administrative measures.

Article 8

1. Member States shall take all necessary steps to ensure that the provisions of occupational schemes contrary to the principle of equal treatment are revised by 1 January 1993.

2. This Directive shall not preclude rights and obligations relating to a period of membership of an occupational scheme prior to revision of that scheme from remaining subject to the provisions of the scheme in force during that period.

Article 9

Member States may defer compulsory application of the principle of equal treatment with regard to:

(a) determination of pensionable age for the purposes of granting old-age or retirement pensions, and the possible implications for other benefits:

— either until the date on which such equality is achieved in statutory schemes,

— or, at the latest, until such equality is required by a directive.

(b) survivors' pensions until a directive requires the principle of equal treatment in statutory social security schemes in that regard;

(c) the application of the first subparagraph of Article 6 (1) (i) to take account of the different actuarial calculation factors, at the latest until the expiry of a thirteen-year period as from the notification of this Directive.

Article 10

Member States shall introduce into their national legal systems such measures as are necessary to enable all persons who consider themselves injured by failure to apply the principle of equal treatment to pursue their claims before the courts, possibly after bringing the matters before other competent authorities.

Article 11

Member States shall take all the necessary steps to protect worker against dismissal where this constitutes a response on the part of the employer to a complaint made at undertaking level or to the institution of legal proceedings aimed at enforcing compliance with the principle of equal treatment.

Article 12

1. Member States shall bring into force such laws, regulations and administrative provisions as are necessary in order to comply with this Directive at the latest three years after notification thereof (¹). They shall immediately inform the Commission thereof.

2. Member States shall communicate to the Commission at the latest five years after notification of this Directive all information necessary to enable the Commission to draw up a report on the application of this Directive for submission to the Council.

Article 13

This Directive is addressed to the Member States.

Done at Brussels, 24 July 1986.

For the Council
The President
A. CLARK

(¹) This Directive was notified to the Member States on 30 July 1986

COUNCIL DIRECTIVE 96/97/EC

of 20 December 1996

amending Directive 86/378/EEC on the implementation of the principle of equal treatment for men and women in occupational social security schemes

THE COUNCIL OF THE EUROPEAN UNION,

Having regard to the Treaty establishing the European Community, and in particular Article 100 thereof,

Having regard to the proposal from the Commission ([1]),

Having regard to the opinion of the European Parliament ([2]),

Having regard to the opinion of the Economic and Social Committee ([3]),

Whereas Article 119 of the Treaty provides that each Member State shall ensure the application of the principle that men and women should receive equal pay for equal work; whereas 'pay' should be taken to mean the ordinary basic or minimum wage or salary and any other consideration, whether in cash or in kind, which the worker receives, directly or indirectly, from his employer in respect of his employment;

Whereas, in its judgement of 17 May 1990, in Case 262/88: Barber v. Guardian Royal Exchange Assurance Group ([4]), the Court of Justice of the European Communities acknowledges that all forms of occupational pension constitute an element of pay within the meaning of Article 119 of the Treaty;

Whereas, in the abovementioned judgment, as clarified by the judgment of 14 December 1993 (Case C-110/91: Moroni v. Collo GmbH) ([5]), the Court interprets Article 119 of the Treaty in such a way that discrimination between men and women in occupational social security schemes is prohibited in general and not only in respect of establishing the age of entitlement to a pension or when an occupational pension is offered by way of compensation for compulsory retirement on economic grounds;

Whereas, in accordance with Protocol 2 concerning Article 119 of the Treaty annexed to the Treaty establishing the European Community, benefits under

occupational social security schemes shall not be considered as remuneration if and in so far as they are attributable to periods of employment prior to 17 May 1990, except in the case of workers or those claiming under them who have, before that date, initiated legal proceedings or raised an equivalent claim under the applicable national law;

Whereas, in its judgments of 28 September 1994 ([6]) (Case C-57/93: Vroege v. NCIV Instituut voor Volkshuisvesting BV and Case C-128/93: Fisscher v. Voorhuis Hengelo BV), the Court ruled that the abovementioned Protocol did not affect the right to join an occupational pension scheme, which continues to be governed by the judgment of 13 May 1986 in Case 170/84: Bilka-Kaufhaus GmbH v. Hartz ([7]), and that the limitation of the effects in time of the judgment of 17 May 1990 in Case C-262/88: Barber v. Guardian Royal Exchange Assurance Group does not apply to the right to join an occupational pension scheme; whereas the Court also ruled that the national rules relating to time limits for bringing actions under national law may be relied on against workers who assert their right to join an occupational pension scheme, provided that they are not less favourable for that type of action than for similar actions of a domestic nature and that they.do not render the exercise of rights conferred by Community law impossible in practice; whereas the Court has also pointed out that the fact that a worker can claim retroactively to join an occupational pension scheme does not allow the worker to avoid paying the contributions relating to the period of membership concerned;

Whereas the exclusion of workers on the grounds of the nature of their work contracts from access to a company or sectorial social security scheme may constitute indirect discrimination against women;

Whereas, in its judgment of 9 November 1993 (Case C-132/92: Birds Eye Walls Ltd v. Friedel M. Roberts) ([8]), the Court has also specified that it is not contrary to Article 119 of the Treaty, when calculating the amount of a bridging pension which is paid by an employer to male and female employees who have taken early retirement on grounds of ill health and which is intended to

([1]) OJ No C 218, 23. 8. 1995, p. 5.
([2]) Opinion delivered on 12 November 1996 (OJ No C 362, 2. 12. 1996).
([3]) OJ No C 18, 22. 1. 1996, p. 132.
([4]) [1990] ECR I-1889.
([5]) [1993] ECR I-6591.

([6]) [1994] ECR I-4541 and (1994) ECR I-4583, respectively.
([7]) [1986] ECR I-1607.
([8]) [1993] ECR I-5579.

17. 2. 97   EN   Official Journal of the European Communities   No L 46/21

compensate, in particular, for loss of income resulting from the fact that they have not yet reached the age required for payment of the State pension which they will subsequently receive and to reduce the amount of the bridging pension accordingly, even though, in the case of men and women aged between 60 and 65, the result is that a female ex-employee receives a smaller bridging pension than that paid to her male counterpart, the difference being equal to the amount of the State pension to which she is entitled as from the age of 60 in respect of the periods of service completed with that employer;

Whereas, in its judgment of 6 October 1993 (Case C-109/91: Ten Oever v. Stichting Bedrijfpensioenfonds voor het Glazenwassers- en Schoonmaakbedrijf) (¹) and in its judgments of 14 December 1993 (Case C-110/91: Moroni v. Collo GmbH), 22 December 1993 (Case C-152/91: Neath v. Hugh Steeper Ltd) (²) and 28 September 1994 (Case C-200/91: Coloroll Pension Trustees Limited v. Russell and Others) (³), the Court confirms that, by virtue of the judgment of 17 May 1990 (Case C-262/88: Barber v. Guardian Royal Exchange Assurance Group), the direct effect of Article 119 of the Treaty may be relied on, for the purpose of claiming equal treatment in the matter of occupational pensions, only in relation to benefits payable in respect of periods of service subsequent to 17 May 1990, except in the case of workers or those claiming under them who have, before that date, initiated legal proceedings or raised an equivalent claim under the applicable national law;

Whereas, in its abovementioned judgments (Case C-109/91: Ten Oever v. Stichting Bedrijfpensioenfonds voor het Glazenwassers- en Schoonmaakbedrijf and Case C-200/91: Coloroll Pension Trustees Limited v. Russell and Others), the Court confirms that the limitation of the effects in time of the Barber judgment applies to survivors' pensions and, consequently, equal treatment in this matter may be claimed only in relation to periods of service subsequent to 17 May 1990, except in the case of those who have, before that date, initiated legal proceedings or raised an equivalent claim under the applicable national law;

Whereas, moreover, in its judgments in Case C-152/91 and Case C-200/91, the Court specifies that the contributions of male and female workers to a defined-benefit pension scheme must be the same, since they are covered by Article 119 of the Treaty, whereas inequality of employers' contributions paid under funded defined-benefit schemes, which is due to the use of actuarial factors differing according to sex, is not to be assessed in the light of that same provision;

Whereas, in its judgments of 28 September 1994 (⁴) (Case C-408/92: Smith v. Advel Systems and Case C-28/93: Van den Akker v. Stichting Shell Pensioenfonds), the Court points out that Article 119 of the Treaty precludes an employer who adopts measures necessary to comply with the Barber judgment of 17 May 1990 (C-262/88) from raising the retirement age for women to that which exists for men in relation to periods of service completed between 17 May 1990 and the date on which those measures come into force; on the other hand, as regards periods of service completed after the latter date, Article 119 does not prevent an employer from taking that step; as regards periods of service prior to 17 May 1990, Community law imposed no obligation which would justify retroactive reduction of the advantages which women enjoyed;

Whereas, in its abovementioned judgment in Case C-200/91: Coloroll Pension Trustees Limited v. Russell and Others), the Court ruled that additional benefits stemming from contributions paid by employees on a purely voluntary basis are not covered by Article 119 of the Treaty;

Whereas, among the measures included in its third medium-term action programme on equal opportunities for women and men (1991 to 1995) (⁵), the Commission emphasizes once more the adoption of suitable measures to take account of the consequences of the judgment of 17 May 1990 in Case 262/88 (Barber v. Guardian Royal Exchange Assurance Group);

Whereas that judgment automatically invalidates certain provisions of Council Directive 86/378/EEC of 24 July 1986 on the implementation of the principle of equal treatment for men and women in occupational social security schemes (⁶) in respect of paid workers;

Whereas Article 119 of the Treaty is directly applicable and can be invoked before the national courts against any employer, whether a private person or a legal person, and whereas it is for these courts to safeguard the rights which that provision confers on individuals;

Whereas, on grounds of legal certainty, it is necessary to amend Directive 86/378/EEC in order to adapt the provisions which are affected by the Barber case-law,

---

(¹) [1993] ECR I-4879.
(²) [1993] ECR I-6953.
(³) [1994] ECR I-4389.

(⁴) [1994] ECR I-4435 and [1994] ECR I-4527, respectively.
(⁵) OJ No C 142, 31. 5. 1991, p. 1.
(⁶) OJ No L 225, 12. 8. 1986, p. 40.

No L 46/22   [EN]   Official Journal of the European Communities   17. 2. 97

HAS ADOPTED THIS DIRECTIVE:

Article 1

Directive 86/378/EEG shall be amended as follows:

1. Article 2 shall be replaced by the following:

'*Article 2*

1. "Occupational social security schemes" means schemes not governed by Directive 79/7/EEC whose purpose is to provide workers, whether employees or self-employed, in an undertaking or group of undertakings, area of economic activity, occupational sector or group of sectors with benefits intended to supplement the benefits provided by statutory social security schemes or to replace them, whether membership of such schemes is compulsory or optional.

2. This Directive does not apply to:

(a) individual contracts for self-employed workers;

(b) schemes for self-employed workers having only one member;

(c) insurance contracts to which the employer is not a party, in the case of salaried workers;

(d) optional provisions of occupational schemes offered to participants individually to guarantee them:
— either additional benefits, or
— a choice of date on which the normal benefits for self-employed workers will start, or a choice between several benefits;

(e) occupational schemes in so far as benefits are financed by contributions paid by workers on a voluntary basis.

3. This Directive does not preclude an employer granting to persons who have already reached the retirement age for the purposes of granting a pension by virtue of an occupational scheme, but who have not yet reached the retirement age for the purposes of granting a statutory retirement pension, a pension supplement, the aim of which is to make equal or more nearly equal the overall amount of benefit paid to these persons in relation to the amount paid to persons of the other sex in the same situation who have already reached the statutory retirement age, until the persons benefiting from the supplement reach the statutory retirement age.'

2. Article 3 shall be replaced by the following:

'*Article 3*

This Directive shall apply to members of the working population, including self-employed persons, persons whose activity is interrupted by illness, maternity, accident or involuntary unemployment and persons seeking employment, to retired and disabled workers and to those claiming under them, in accordance with national law and/or practice.'

3. Article 6 shall be replaced by the following:

'*Article 6*

1. Provisions contrary to the principle of equal treatment shall include those based on sex, either directly or indirectly, in particular by reference to marital or family status, for:

(a) determining the persons who may participate in an occupational scheme;

(b) fixing the compulsory or optional nature of participation in an occupational scheme;

(c) laying down different rules as regards the age of entry into the scheme or the minimum period of employment or membership of the scheme required to obtain the benefits thereof;

(d) laying down different rules, except as provided for in points (h) and (i), for the reimbursement of contributions when a worker leaves a scheme without having fulfilled the conditions guaranteeing a deferred right to long-term benefits;

(e) setting different conditions for the granting of benefits or restricting such benefits to workers of one or other of the sexes;

(f) fixing different retirement ages;

(g) suspending the retention or acquisition of rights during periods of maternity leave or leave for family reasons which are granted by law or agreement and are paid by the employer;

(h) setting different levels of benefit, except in so far as may be necessary to take account of actuarial calculation factors which differ according to sex in the case of defined-contribution schemes.

17. 2. 97   EN   Official Journal of the European Communities   No L 46/23

In the case of funded defined-benefit schemes, certain elements (examples of which are annexed) may be unequal where the inequality of the amounts results from the effects of the use of actuarial factors differing according to sex at the time when the scheme's funding is implemented;

(i) setting different levels for workers' contributions;

setting different levels for employers' contributions, except:

— in the case of defined-contribution schemes if the aim is to equalize the amount of the final benefits or to make them more nearly equal for both sexes,

— in the case of funded defined-benefit schemes where the employer's contributions are intended to ensure the adequacy of the funds necessary to cover the cost of the benefits defined,

(j) laying down different standards or standards applicable only to workers of a specified sex, except as provided for in points (h) and (i), as regards the guarantee or retention of entitlement to deferred benefits when a worker leaves a scheme.

2. Where the granting of benefits within the scope of this Directive is left to the discretion of the scheme's management bodies, the latter must comply with the principle of equal treatment.'

4. Article 8 shall be replaced by the following:

'*Article 8*

1. Member States shall take the necessary steps to ensure that the provisions of occupational schemes for self-employed workers contrary to the principle of equal treatment are revised with effect from 1 January 1993 at the latest.

2. This Directive shall not preclude rights and obligations relating to a period of membership of an occupational scheme for self-employed workers prior to revision of that scheme from remaining subject to the provisions of the scheme in force during that period.'

5. Article 9 shall be replaced by the following:

'*Article 9*

As regards schemes for self-employed workers, Member States may defer compulsory application of the principle of equal treatment with regard to:

(a) determination of pensionable age for the granting of old-age or retirement pensions, and the possible implications for other benefits:

— either until the date on which such equality is achieved in statutory schemes,

— or, at the latest, until such equality is prescribed by a directive;

(b) survivors' pensions until Community law establishes the principle of equal treatment in statutory social security schemes in that regard;

(c) the application of the first subparagraph of point (i) of Article 6 (1) to take account of the different actuarial calculation factors, at the latest until 1 January 1999.'

6. The following Article shall be inserted:

'*Article 9a*

Where men and women may claim a flexible pensionable age under the same conditions, this shall not be deemed to be incompatible with this Directive.'

7. The following Annex shall be added:

'ANNEX

Examples of elements which may be unequal, in respect of funded defined-benefit schemes, as referred to in Article 6 (h):

— conversion into a capital sum of part of a periodic pension,

— transfer of pension rights,

— a reversionary pension payable to a dependant in return for the surrender of part of a pension,

— a reduced pension where the worker opts to take early retirement.'

Article 2

1. Any measure implementing this Directive, as regards paid workers, must cover all benefits derived from periods of employment subsequent to 17 May 1990 and shall apply retroactively to that date, without prejudice to workers or those claiming under them who have, before that date, initiated legal proceedings or raised an equivalent claim under national law. In that event, the implementation measures must apply retroactively to 8 April 1976 and must cover all the benefits derived from periods of employment after that date. For Member States which acceded to the Community after 8 April 1976, that date shall be replaced by the date on which Article 119 of the Treaty became applicable on their territory.

No L 46/24   EN   Official Journal of the European Communities   17. 2. 97

2. The second sentence of paragraph 1 shall not prevent national rules relating to time limits for bringing actions under national law from being relied on against workers or those claiming under them who initiated legal proceedings or raise an equivalent claim under national law before 17 May 1990, provided that they are not less favourable for that type of action than for similar actions of a domestic nature and that they do not render the exercise of Community law impossible in practice.

3. For Member States whose accession took place after 17 May 1990 and who were on 1 January 1994 Contracting Parties to the Agreement on the European Economic Area, the date of 17 May 1990 in paragraph 1 and 2 of this Directive is replaced by 1 January 1994.

Article 3

1. Member States shall bring into force the laws, regulations and administrative provisions necessary to comply with this Directive by 1 July 1997. They shall forthwith inform the Commission thereof.

When Member States adopt these provisions, they shall contain a reference to this Directive or be accompanied by such reference on the occasion of their official publication. The methods of making such a reference shall be laid down by the Member States.

2. Member States shall communicate to the Commission, at the latest two years after the entry into force of this Directive, all information necessary to enable the Commission to draw up a report on the application of this Directive.

Article 4

This Directive shall enter into force on the 20 day following that of its publication in the *Official Journal of the European Communities.*

Article 5

This Directive is addressed to the Member States.

Done at Brussels, 20 December 1996.

For the Council

The President

S. BARRETT

18. 6. 1999   EN   Official Journal of the European Communities   L 151/39

CORRIGENDA

Corrigendum to Council Regulation (EC) No 3290/94 of 22 December 1994 on the adjustments and transitional arrangements required in the agriculture sector in order to implement the agreements concluded during the Uruguay Round of multilateral trade negotiations

(Official Journal of the European Communities L 349 of 31 December 1994)

On page 129, in Annex IV, SUGAR (Replacement of Title II of Regulation (EEC) No 1785/81), Article 17a(2)(b), second indent:

for: 'from the areas referred to in (a) ...',

read: 'from the areas referred to in the first indent ...'.

———————

Corrigendum to Council Directive 96/97/EC of 20 December 1996 amending Directive 86/378/EEC on the implementation of the principle of equal treatment for men and women in occupational social security schemes

(Official Journal of the European Communities L 46 of 17 February 1997)

On page 23, in Article 2(1), last sentence:

for: 'For Member States which acceded to the Community after 8 April 1976, ...',

read: 'For Member States which acceded to the Community after 8 April 1976, and before 17 May 1990,'.

On page 24, in Article 2(3):

for: '... the date of 17 May 1990 in paragraph 1 and 2 of the Directive is replaced ...',

read: '... the date of 17 May 1990 in the first sentence of paragraph 1 of this Article is replaced ...'.

———————

L 14/6   EN   Official Journal of the European Communities   20. 1. 98

COUNCIL DIRECTIVE 97/80/EC
of 15 December 1997
on the burden of proof in cases of discrimination based on sex

THE COUNCIL OF THE EUROPEAN UNION,

Having regard to the Agreement on social policy annexed to the Protocol (No 14) on social policy annexed to the Treaty establishing the European Community, and in particular Article 2(2) thereof,

Having regard to the proposal from the Commission (¹),

Having regard to the opinion of the Economic and Social Committee (²),

Acting, in accordance with the procedure laid down in Article 189c of the Treaty, in cooperation with the European Parliament (³),

(1) Whereas, on the basis of the Protocol on social policy annexed to the Treaty, the Member States, with the exception of the United Kingdom of Great Britain and Northern Ireland (hereinafter called 'the Member States'), wishing to implement the 1989 Social Charter, have concluded an Agreement on social policy;

(2) Whereas the Community Charter of the Fundamental Social Rights of Workers recognizes the importance of combating every form of discrimination, including discrimination on grounds of sex, colour, race, opinions and beliefs;

(3) Whereas paragraph 16 of the Community Charter of the Fundamental Social Rights of Workers on equal treatment for men and women, provides, *inter alia*, that 'action should be intensified to ensure the implementation of the principle of equality for men and women as regards, in particular, access to employment, remuneration, working conditions, social protection, education, vocational training and career development';

(4) Whereas, in accordance with Article 3(2) of the Agreement on social policy, the Commission has consulted management and labour at Community level on the possible direction of Community action on the burden of proof in cases of discrimination based on sex;

(5) Whereas the Commission, considering Community action advisable after such consultation, once again consulted management and labour on the content of the proposal contemplated in accordance with Article 3(3) of the same Agreement; whereas the latter have sent their opinions to the Commission;

(6) Whereas, after the second round of consultation, neither management nor labour have informed the Commission of their wish to initiate the process — possibly leading to an agreement — provided for in Article 4 of the same Agreement;

(7) Whereas, in accordance with Article 1 of the Agreement, the Community and the Member States have set themselves the objective, *inter alia*, of improving living and working conditions; whereas effective implementation of the principle of equal treatment for men and women would contribute to the achievement of that aim;

(8) Whereas the principle of equal treatment was stated in Article 119 of the Treaty, in Council Directive 75/117/EEC of 10 February 1975 on the approximation of the laws of the Member States relating to the application of the principle of equal pay for men and women (⁴) and in Council Directive 76/207/EEC of 9 February 1976 on the implementation of the principle of equal treatment for men and women as regards access to employment, vocational training and promotion and working conditions (⁵);

(9) Whereas Council Directive 92/85/EEC of 19 October 1992 on the introduction of measures to encourage improvements in the safety and health at work of pregnant workers and workers who have recently given birth or are breastfeeding (⁶) also contributes to the effective implementation of the principle of equal treatment for men and women; whereas that Directive should not work to the detriment of the aforementioned Directives on equal treatment; whereas, therefore, female workers covered by that Directive should likewise benefit from the adaptation of the rules on the burden of proof;

(¹) OJ C 332, 7. 11. 1996, p. 11 and
   OJ C 185, 18. 6. 1997, p. 21.
(²) OJ C 133, 28. 4. 1997, p. 34.
(³) Opinion of the European Parliament of 10 April 1997 (OJ C 132, 28. 4. 1997, p. 215), Common Position of the Council of 24 July 1997 (OJ C 307, 8. 10. 1997, p. 6) and Decision of the European Parliament of 6 November 1997 (OJ C 358, 24. 11. 1997).

(⁴) OJ L 45, 19. 2. 1975, p. 19.
(⁵) OJ L 39, 14. 2. 1976, p. 40.
(⁶) OJ L 348, 28. 11. 1992, p. 1.

20. 1. 98 | EN | Official Journal of the European Communities | L 14/7

(10) Whereas Council Directive 96/34/EC of 3 June 1996 on the framework agreement on parental leave concluded by UNICE, CEEP and the ETUC(¹), is also based on the principle of equal treatment for men and women;

(11) Whereas the references to 'judicial process' and 'court' cover mechanisms by means of which disputes may be submitted for examination and decision to independent bodies which may hand down decisions that are binding on the parties to those disputes;

(12) Whereas the expression 'out-of-court procedures' means in particular procedures such as conciliation and mediation;

(13) Whereas the appreciation of the facts from which it may be presumed that there has been direct or indirect discrimination is a matter for national judicial or other competent bodies, in accordance with national law or practice;

(14) Whereas it is for the Member States to introduce, at any appropriate stage of the proceedings, rules of evidence which are more favourable to plaintiffs;

(15) Whereas it is necessary to take account of the specific features of certain Member States' legal systems, *inter alia* where an inference of discrimination is drawn if the respondent fails to produce evidence that satisfies the court or other competent authority that there has been no breach of the principle of equal treatment;

(16) Whereas Member States need not apply the rules on the burden of proof to proceedings in which it is for the court or other competent body to investigate the facts of the case; whereas the procedures thus referred to are those in which the plaintiff is not required to prove the facts, which it is for the court or competent body to investigate;

(17) Whereas plaintiffs could be deprived of any effective means of enforcing the principle of equal treatment before the national courts if the effect of introducing evidence of an apparent discrimination were not to impose upon the respondent the burden of proving that his practice is not in fact discriminatory;

(18) Whereas the Court of Justice of the European Communities has therefore held that the rules on the burden of proof must be adapted when there is a prima facie case of discrimination and that, for the principle of equal treatment to be applied effectively, the burden of proof must shift back to the

(¹) OJ L 145, 19. 6. 1996, p. 4.

respondent when evidence of such discrimination is brought;

(19) Whereas it is all the more difficult to prove discrimination when it is indirect; whereas it is therefore important to define indirect discrimination;

(20) Whereas the aim of adequately adapting the rules on the burden of proof has not been achieved satisfactorily in all Member States and, in accordance with the principle of subsidiarity stated in Article 3b of the Treaty and with that of proportionality, that aim must be attained at Community level; whereas this Directive confines itself to the minimum action required and does not go beyond what is necessary for that purpose,

HAS ADOPTED THIS DIRECTIVE:

Article 1

Aim

The aim of this Directive shall be to ensure that the measures taken by the Member States to implement the principle of equal treatment are made more effective, in order to enable all persons who consider themselves wronged because the principle of equal treatment has not been applied to them to have their rights asserted by judicial process after possible recourse to other competent bodies.

Article 2

Definitions

1. For the purposes of this Directive, the principle of equal treatment shall mean that there shall be no discrimination whatsoever based on sex, either directly or indirectly.

2. For purposes of the principle of equal treatment referred to in paragraph 1, indirect discrimination shall exist where an apparently neutral provision, criterion or practice disadvantages a substantially higher proportion of the members of one sex unless that provision, criterion or practice is appropriate and necessary and can be justified by objective factors unrelated to sex.

Article 3

Scope

1. This Directive shall apply to:

(a) the situations covered by Article 119 of the Treaty and by Directives 75/117/EEC, 76/207/EEC and, insofar as discrimination based on sex is concerned, 92/85/EEC and 96/34/EC;

(b) any civil or administrative procedure concerning the public or private sector which provides for means of redress under national law pursuant to the measures referred to in (a) with the exception of out-of-court procedures of a voluntary nature or provided for in national law.

2. This Directive shall not apply to criminal procedures, unless otherwise provided by the Member States.

Article 4

Burden of proof

1. Member States shall take such measures as are necessary, in accordance with their national judicial systems, to ensure that, when persons who consider themselves wronged because the principle of equal treatment has not been applied to them establish, before a court or other competent authority, facts from which it may be presumed that there has been direct or indirect discrimination, it shall be for the respondent to prove that there has been no breach of the principle of equal treatment.

2. This Directive shall not prevent Member States from introducing rules of evidence which are more favourable to plaintiffs.

3. Member States need not apply paragraph 1 to proceedings in which it is for the court or competent body to investigate the facts of the case.

Article 5

Information

Member States shall ensure that measures taken pursuant to this Directive, together with the provisions already in force, are brought to the attention of all the persons concerned by all appropriate means.

Article 6

Non-regression

Implementation of this Directive shall under no circumstances be sufficient grounds for a reduction in the general level of protection of workers in the areas to which it applies, without prejudice to the Member States' right to respond to changes in the situation by introducing laws, regulations and administrative provisions which differ from those in force on the notification of this Directive, provided that the minimum requirements of this Directive are complied with.

Article 7

Implementation

The Member States shall bring into force the laws, regulations and administrative provisions necessary for them to comply with this Directive by 1 January 2001. They shall immediately inform the Commission thereof.

When the Member States adopt those measures they shall contain a reference to this Directive or shall be accompanied by such a reference on the occasion of their official publication. The methods of making such references shall be laid down by the Member States.

The Member States shall communicate to the Commission, within two years of the entry into force of this Directive, all the information necessary for the Commission to draw up a report to the European Parliament and the Council on the application of this Directive.

Article 8

This Directive is addressed to the Member States.

Done at Brussels, 15 December 1997.

For the Council
The President
J.-C. JUNCKER

5.10.2002   EN   Official Journal of the European Communities   L 269/15

DIRECTIVE 2002/73/EC OF THE EUROPEAN PARLIAMENT AND OF THE COUNCIL

of 23 September 2002

amending Council Directive 76/207/EEC on the implementation of the principle of equal treatment for men and women as regards access to employment, vocational training and promotion, and working conditions

(Text with EEA relevance)

THE EUROPEAN PARLIAMENT AND THE COUNCIL OF THE EUROPEAN UNION,

Having regard to the Treaty establishing the European Community and, in particular, Article 141(3) thereof,

Having regard to the proposal from the Commission (¹),

Having regard to the Opinion of the Economic and Social Committee (²),

Acting in accordance with the procedure laid down in Article 251 of the Treaty (³), in the light of the joint text approved by the Conciliation Committee on 19 April 2002,

Whereas:

(1) In accordance with Article 6 of the Treaty on European Union, the European Union is founded on the principles of liberty, democracy, respect for human rights and fundamental freedoms, and the rule of law, principles which are common to the Member States, and shall respect fundamental rights as guaranteed by the European Convention for the Protection of Human Rights and Fundamental Freedoms and as they result from the constitutional traditions common to the Member States, as general principles of Community law.

(2) The right to equality before the law and protection against discrimination for all persons constitutes a universal right recognised by the Universal Declaration of Human Rights, the United Nations Convention on the Elimination of all forms of Discrimination Against Women, the International Convention on the Elimination of all Forms of Racial Discrimination and the United Nations Covenants on Civil and Political Rights and on Economic, Social and Cultural Rights and by the Convention for the Protection of Human Rights and Fundamental Freedoms, to which all Member States are signatories.

(3) This Directive respects the fundamental rights and observes the principles recognised in particular by the Charter of Fundamental Rights of the European Union.

(4) Equality between women and men is a fundamental principle, under Article 2 and Article 3(2) of the EC Treaty and the case-law of the Court of Justice. These Treaty provisions proclaim equality between women and men as a 'task' and an 'aim' of the Community and impose a positive obligation to 'promote' it in all its activities.

(5) Article 141 of the Treaty, and in particular paragraph 3, addresses specifically equal opportunities and equal treatment of men and women in matters of employment and occupation.

(6) Council Directive 76/207/EEC (⁴) does not define the concepts of direct or indirect discrimination. On the basis of Article 13 of the Treaty, the Council has adopted Directive 2000/43/EC of 29 June 2000 implementing the principle of equal treatment between persons irrespective of racial or ethnic origin (⁵) and Directive 2000/78/EC of 27 November 2000 establishing a general framework for equal treatment in employment and occupation (⁶) which define direct and indirect discrimination. Thus it is appropriate to insert definitions consistent with these Directives in respect of sex.

(7) This Directive does not prejudice freedom of association, including the right to establish unions with others and to join unions to defend one's interests. Measures within the meaning of Article 141(4) of the Treaty may include membership or the continuation of the activity of organisations or unions whose main objective is the promotion, in practice, of the principle of equal treatment between women and men.

(8) Harassment related to the sex of a person and sexual harassment are contrary to the principle of equal treatment between women and men; it is therefore appropriate to define such concepts and to prohibit such forms of discrimination. To this end it must be emphasised that these forms of discrimination occur not only in the workplace, but also in the context of access to employment and vocational training, during employment and occupation.

(9) In this context, employers and those responsible for vocational training should be encouraged to take measures to combat all forms of sexual discrimination and, in

---

(¹) OJ C 337 E, 28.11.2000, p. 204 and OJ C 270 E, 25.9.2001, p. 9.
(²) OJ C 123, 25.4.2001, p. 81.
(³) Opinion of the European Parliament of 31 May 2001 (OJ C 47, 21.2.2002, p. 19), Council Common Position of 23 July 2001 (OJ C 307, 31.10.2001, p. 5) and Decision of the European Parliament of 24 October 2001 (OJ C 112 E, 9.5.2002, p. 14). Decision of the European Parliament of 12 June 2002 and Council Decision of 13 June 2002.

(⁴) OJ L 39, 14.2.1976, p. 40.
(⁵) OJ L 180, 19.7.2000, p. 22.
(⁶) OJ L 303, 2.12.2000, p. 16.

particular, to take preventive measures against harassment and sexual harassment in the workplace, in accordance with national legislation and practice.

(10) The appreciation of the facts from which it may be inferred that there has been direct or indirect discrimination is a matter for national judicial or other competent bodies, in accordance with rules of national law or practice. Such rules may provide in particular for indirect discrimination to be established by any means including on the basis of statistical evidence. According to the case-law of the Court of Justice (¹), discrimination involves the application of different rules to a comparable situation or the application of the same rule to different situations.

(11) The occupational activities that Member States may exclude from the scope of Directive 76/207/EEC should be restricted to those which necessitate the employment of a person of one sex by reason of the nature of the particular occupational activities concerned, provided that the objective sought is legitimate, and subject to the principle of proportionality as laid down by the case-law of the Court of Justice (²).

(12) The Court of Justice has consistently recognised the legitimacy, in terms of the principle of equal treatment, of protecting a woman's biological condition during and after pregnancy. It has moreover consistently ruled that any unfavourable treatment of women related to pregnancy or maternity constitutes direct sex discrimination. This Directive is therefore without prejudice to Council Directive 92/85/EEC of 19 October 1992 on the introduction of measures to encourage improvements in the safety and health at work of pregnant workers and workers who have recently given birth or are breastfeeding (³) (tenth individual Directive within the meaning of Article 16(1) of Directive 89/391/EEC), which aims to ensure the protection of the physical and mental state of women who are pregnant, women who have recently given birth or women who are breastfeeding. The preamble to Directive 92/85/EEC provides that the protection of the safety and health of pregnant workers, workers who have recently given birth or workers who are breastfeeding should not involve treating women who are on the labour market unfavourably nor work to the detriment of Directives concerning equal treatment for men and women. The Court of Justice has recognised the protection of employment rights of women, in particular their right to return to the same or an equivalent job, with no less favourable working conditions, as well as to benefit from any improvement in working

conditions to which they would be entitled during their absence.

(13) In the Resolution of the Council and of the Ministers for Employment and Social Policy meeting within the Council of 29 June 2000 on the balanced participation of women and men in family and working life (⁴), Member States were encouraged to consider examining the scope for their respective legal systems to grant working men an individual and untransferable right to paternity leave, while maintaining their rights relating to employment. In this context, it is important to stress that it is for the Member States to determine whether or not to grant such a right and also to determine any conditions, other than dismissal and return to work, which are outside the scope of this Directive.

(14) Member States may, under Article 141(4) of the Treaty, maintain or adopt measures providing for specific advantages, in order to make it easier for the under-represented sex to pursue a vocational activity or to prevent or compensate for disadvantages in professional careers. Given the current situation, and bearing in mind Declaration No 28 to the Amsterdam Treaty, Members States should, in the first instance, aim at improving the situation of women in working life.

(15) The prohibition of discrimination should be without prejudice to the maintenance or adoption of measures intended to prevent or compensate for disadvantages suffered by a group of persons of one sex. Such measures permit organisations of persons of one sex where their main object is the promotion of the special needs of those persons and the promotion of equality between women and men.

(16) The principle of equal pay for men and women is already firmly established by Article 141 of the Treaty and Council Directive 75/117/EEC of 10 February 1975 on the approximation of the laws of the Member States relating to the application of the principle of equal pay for men and women (⁵) and is consistently upheld by the case-law of the Court of Justice; the principle constitutes an essential and indispensable part of the *acquis communautaire* concerning sex discrimination.

(17) The Court of Justice has ruled that, having regard to the fundamental nature of the right to effective judicial protection, employees enjoy such protection even after the employment relationship has ended (⁶). An employee defending or giving evidence on behalf of a person protected under this Directive should be entitled to the same protection.

(¹) Case C-394/96 Brown, [1998] ECR I-4185, Case C-342/93 Gillespie, [1996] ECR I-475.
(²) Case C-222/84 Johnston, [1986] ECR 1651, Case C-273/97 Sirdar [1999] ECR I-7403 and Case C-285/98 Kreil [2000] ECR I-69.
(³) OJ L 348, 28.11.1992, p. 1.

(⁴) OJ C 218, 31.7.2000, p. 5.
(⁵) OJ L 45, 19.2.1975, p. 19.
(⁶) Case C-185/97 Coote [1998] ECR I-5199.

5.10.2002   EN   Official Journal of the European Communities   L 269/17

(18) The Court of Justice has ruled that, in order to be effective, the principle of equal treatment implies that, whenever it is breached, the compensation awarded to the employee discriminated against must be adequate in relation to the damage sustained. It has furthermore specified that fixing a prior upper limit may preclude effective compensation and that excluding an award of interest to compensate for the loss sustained is not allowed (¹).

(19) According to the case-law of the Court of Justice, national rules relating to time limits for bringing actions are admissible provided that they are not less favourable than time limits for similar actions of a domestic nature and that they do not render the exercise of rights conferred by the Community law impossible in practice.

(20) Persons who have been subject to discrimination based on sex should have adequate means of legal protection. To provide a more effective level of protection, associations, organisations and other legal entities should also be empowered to engage in proceedings, as the Member States so determine, either on behalf or in support of any victim, without prejudice to national rules of procedure concerning representation and defence before the courts.

(21) Member States should promote dialogue between the social partners and, within the framework of national practice, with non-governmental organisations to address different forms of discrimination based on sex in the workplace and to combat them.

(22) Member States should provide for effective, proportionate and dissuasive sanctions in case of breaches of the obligations under Directive 76/207/EEC.

(23) In accordance with the principle of subsidiarity as set out in Article 5 of the Treaty, the objectives of the proposed action cannot be sufficiently achieved by the Member States and can therefore be better achieved by the Community. In accordance with the principle of proportionality, as set out in that Article, this Directive does not go beyond what is necessary for that purpose.

(24) Directive 76/207/EEC should therefore be amended accordingly,

HAVE ADOPTED THIS DIRECTIVE:

Article 1

Directive 76/207/EEC is hereby amended as follows:

1. in Article 1, the following paragraph shall be inserted:

'1a. Member States shall actively take into account the objective of equality between men and women when formulating and implementing laws, regulations, administrative

provisions, policies and activities in the areas referred to in paragraph 1.';

2. Article 2 shall be replaced by the following:

'*Article 2*

1. For the purposes of the following provisions, the principle of equal treatment shall mean that there shall be no discrimination whatsoever on grounds of sex either directly or indirectly by reference in particular to marital or family status.

2. For the purposes of this Directive, the following definitions shall apply:

— direct discrimination: where one person is treated less favourably on grounds of sex than another is, has been or would be treated in a comparable situation,

— indirect discrimination: where an apparently neutral provision, criterion or practice would put persons of one sex at a particular disadvantage compared with persons of the other sex, unless that provision, criterion or practice is objectively justified by a legitimate aim, and the means of achieving that aim are appropriate and necessary,

— harassment: where an unwanted conduct related to the sex of a person occurs with the purpose or effect of violating the dignity of a person, and of creating an intimidating, hostile, degrading, humiliating or offensive environment,

— sexual harassment: where any form of unwanted verbal, non-verbal or physical conduct of a sexual nature occurs, with the purpose or effect of violating the dignity of a person, in particular when creating an intimidating, hostile, degrading, humiliating or offensive environment.

3. Harassment and sexual harassment within the meaning of this Directive shall be deemed to be discrimination on the grounds of sex and therefore prohibited.

A person's rejection of, or submission to, such conduct may not be used as a basis for a decision affecting that person.

4. An instruction to discriminate against persons on grounds of sex shall be deemed to be discrimination within the meaning of this Directive.

5. Member States shall encourage, in accordance with national law, collective agreements or practice, employers and those responsible for access to vocational training to take measures to prevent all forms of discrimination on grounds of sex, in particular harassment and sexual harassment at the workplace.

(¹) Case C-180/95, Draehmpaehl, [1997] ECR I-2195, Case C-271/91, Marshall [1993] ECR I-4367.

6. Member States may provide, as regards access to employment including the training leading thereto, that a difference of treatment which is based on a characteristic related to sex shall not constitute discrimination where, by reason of the nature of the particular occupational activities concerned or of the context in which they are carried out, such a characteristic constitutes a genuine and determining occupational requirement, provided that the objective is legitimate and the requirement is proportionate.

7. This Directive shall be without prejudice to provisions concerning the protection of women, particularly as regards pregnancy and maternity.

A woman on maternity leave shall be entitled, after the end of her period of maternity leave, to return to her job or to an equivalent post on terms and conditions which are no less favourable to her and to benefit from any improvement in working conditions to which she would be entitled during her absence.

Less favourable treatment of a woman related to pregnancy or maternity leave within the meaning of Directive 92/85/EEC shall constitute discrimination within the meaning of this Directive.

This Directive shall also be without prejudice to the provisions of Council Directive 96/34/EC of 3 June 1996 on the framework agreement on parental leave concluded by UNICE, CEEP and the ETUC (*) and of Council Directive 92/85/EEC of 19 October 1992 on the introduction of measures to encourage improvements in the safety and health at work of pregnant workers and workers who have recently given birth or are breastfeeding (tenth individual Directive within the meaning of Article 16(1) of Directive 89/391/EEC) (**). It is also without prejudice to the right of Member States to recognise distinct rights to paternity and/or adoption leave. Those Member States which recognise such rights shall take the necessary measures to protect working men and women against dismissal due to exercising those rights and ensure that, at the end of such leave, they shall be entitled to return to their jobs or to equivalent posts on terms and conditions which are no less favourable to them, and to benefit from any improvement in working conditions to which they would have been entitled during their absence.

8. Member States may maintain or adopt measures within the meaning of Article 141(4) of the Treaty with a view to ensuring full equality in practice between men and women.

(*) OJ L 145, 19.6.1996, p. 4.
(**) OJ L 348, 28.11.1992, p. 1.';

3. Article 3 shall be replaced by the following:

'*Article 3*

1. Application of the principle of equal treatment means that there shall be no direct or indirect discrimination on the grounds of sex in the public or private sectors, including public bodies, in relation to:

(a) conditions for access to employment, to self-employment or to occupation, including selection criteria and recruitment conditions, whatever the branch of activity and at all levels of the professional hierarchy, including promotion;

(b) access to all types and to all levels of vocational guidance, vocational training, advanced vocational training and retraining, including practical work experience;

(c) employment and working conditions, including dismissals, as well as pay as provided for in Directive 75/117/EEC;

(d) membership of, and involvement in, an organisation of workers or employers, or any organisation whose members carry on a particular profession, including the benefits provided for by such organisations.

2. To that end, Member States shall take the necessary measures to ensure that:

(a) any laws, regulations and administrative provisions contrary to the principle of equal treatment are abolished;

(b) any provisions contrary to the principle of equal treatment which are included in contracts or collective agreements, internal rules of undertakings or rules governing the independent occupations and professions and workers' and employers' organisations shall be, or may be declared, null and void or are amended.';

4. Articles 4 and 5 shall be deleted;

5. Article 6 shall be replaced by the following:

'*Article 6*

1. Member States shall ensure that judicial and/or administrative procedures, including where they deem it appropriate conciliation procedures, for the enforcement of obligations under this Directive are available to all persons who consider themselves wronged by failure to apply the principle of equal treatment to them, even after the relationship in which the discrimination is alleged to have occurred has ended.

2. Member States shall introduce into their national legal systems such measures as are necessary to ensure real and effective compensation or reparation as the Member States so determine for the loss and damage sustained by a person injured as a result of discrimination contrary to Article 3, in a way which is dissuasive and proportionate to the damage suffered; such compensation or reparation may not be restricted by the fixing of a prior upper limit, except in cases where the employer can prove that the only damage suffered by an applicant as a result of discrimination within the meaning of this Directive is the refusal to take his/her job application into consideration.

5.10.2002 | EN | Official Journal of the European Communities | L 269/19

3. Member States shall ensure that associations, organisations or other legal entities which have, in accordance with the criteria laid down by their national law, a legitimate interest in ensuring that the provisions of this Directive are complied with, may engage, either on behalf or in support of the complainants, with his or her approval, in any judicial and/or administrative procedure provided for the enforcement of obligations under this Directive.

4. Paragraphs 1 and 3 are without prejudice to national rules relating to time limits for bringing actions as regards the principle of equal treatment.';

6. Article 7 shall be replaced by the following:

'*Article 7*

Member States shall introduce into their national legal systems such measures as are necessary to protect employees, including those who are employees' representatives provided for by national laws and/or practices, against dismissal or other adverse treatment by the employer as a reaction to a complaint within the undertaking or to any legal proceedings aimed at enforcing compliance with the principle of equal treatment.';

7. the following Articles shall be inserted:

'*Article 8a*

1. Member States shall designate and make the necessary arrangements for a body or bodies for the promotion, analysis, monitoring and support of equal treatment of all persons without discrimination on the grounds of sex. These bodies may form part of agencies charged at national level with the defence of human rights or the safeguard of individuals' rights.

2. Member States shall ensure that the competences of these bodies include:

(a) without prejudice to the right of victims and of associations, organisations or other legal entities referred to in Article 6(3), providing independent assistance to victims of discrimination in pursuing their complaints about discrimination;

(b) conducting independent surveys concerning discrimination;

(c) publishing independent reports and making recommendations on any issue relating to such discrimination.

Article 8b

1. Member States shall, in accordance with national traditions and practice, take adequate measures to promote social dialogue between the social partners with a view to fostering equal treatment, including through the monitoring of workplace practices, collective agreements, codes of conduct, research or exchange of experiences and good practices.

2. Where consistent with national traditions and practice, Member States shall encourage the social partners, without prejudice to their autonomy, to promote equality between women and men and to conclude, at the appropriate level, agreements laying down anti-discrimination rules in the fields referred to in Article 1 which fall within the scope of collective bargaining. These agreements shall respect the minimum requirements laid down by this Directive and the relevant national implementing measures.

3. Member States shall, in accordance with national law, collective agreements or practice, encourage employers to promote equal treatment for men and women in the workplace in a planned and systematic way.

4. To this end, employers should be encouraged to provide at appropriate regular intervals employees and/or their representatives with appropriate information on equal treatment for men and women in the undertaking.

Such information may include statistics on proportions of men and women at different levels of the organisation and possible measures to improve the situation in cooperation with employees' representatives.

Article 8c

Member States shall encourage dialogue with appropriate non-governmental organisations which have, in accordance with their national law and practice, a legitimate interest in contributing to the fight against discrimination on grounds of sex with a view to promoting the principle of equal treatment.

Article 8d

Member States shall lay down the rules on sanctions applicable to infringements of the national provisions adopted pursuant to this Directive, and shall take all measures necessary to ensure that they are applied.

The sanctions, which may comprise the payment of compensation to the victim, must be effective, proportionate and dissuasive. The Member States shall notify those provisions to the Commission by 5 October 2005 at the latest and shall notify it without delay of any subsequent amendment affecting them.

Article 8e

1. Member States may introduce or maintain provisions which are more favourable to the protection of the principle of equal treatment than those laid down in this Directive.

2. The implementation of this Directive shall under no circumstances constitute grounds for a reduction in the level of protection against discrimination already afforded by Member States in the fields covered by this Directive.'

L 269/20   EN   Official Journal of the European Communities   5.10.2002

Article 2

1. Member States shall bring into force the laws, regulations and administrative provisions necessary to comply with this Directive by 5 October 2005 at the latest or shall ensure, by that date at the latest, that management and labour introduce the requisite provisions by way of agreement. Member States shall take all necessary steps to enable them at all times to guarantee the results imposed by this Directive. They shall immediately inform the Commission thereof.

When Member States adopt those measures, they shall contain a reference to this Directive or be accompanied by such reference on the occasion of their official publication. Member States shall determine how such reference is to be made.

2. The Member States shall communicate to the Commission, within three years of the entry into force of this Directive, all the information necessary for the Commission to draw up a report to the European Parliament and the Council on the application of this Directive.

3. Without prejudice to paragraph 2, Member States shall communicate to the Commission, every four years, the texts of laws, regulations and administrative provisions of any measures adopted pursuant to Article 141(4) of the Treaty, as well as reports on these measures and their implementation. On the basis of that information, the Commission will adopt and publish every four years a report establishing a comparative assessment of any measures in the light of Declaration No 28 annexed to the Final Act of the Treaty of Amsterdam.

Article 3

This Directive shall enter into force on the day of its publication in the *Official Journal of the European Communities*.

Article 4

This Directive is addressed to the Member States.

Done at Brussels, 23 September 2002.

For the European Parliament	For the Council
The President	The President
P. COX	M. FISCHER BOEL